D0762942

GRAMMAR AND WRITING

FOR JOB AND PERSONAL USE

Joyce Hing-McGowan

Director of Career-Vocational Education
Program Improvement / Certification Systems
Sonoma State University
Rohnert Park, California

Merle Wood

Education Consultant
Formerly of Oakland Public Schools
Lafayette, California

South-Western Publishing Co.

Acquisitions Editor: Karen Schneiter
Series Editor: Mark Linton
Editorial Production Manager: Linda R. Allen
Production Editor: Karen Roberts
Designer: Darren Wright
Production Artist: Steven McMahon
Photo Editor/Stylist: Devore M. Nixon
Marketing Manager: Shelly Battenfield
Cover Photo: (c) Robert Hale

South-Western Publishing Co. gratefully acknowledges the foresight and commitment
that Ben Willard, Acquisitions Editor, gave to this LIFE Series.

Copyright (C) 1992
by SOUTH-WESTERN PUBLISHING CO.
Cincinnati, Ohio

ALL RIGHTS RESERVED
The text of this publication, or any part thereof, may not be reproduced or transmitted
in any form or by any means, electronic or mechanical, including photocopying, recording, storage in an information retrieval system, or otherwise, without the prior written
permission of the publisher.

Library of Congress Cataloging-in-Publication Data

Hing-McGowan, Joyce.
        Grammar and writing for job and personal use / Joyce Hing-McGowan, Merle
        Wood.
        p.   cm.
        Includes index.
        ISBN 0-538-70479-9
        1. English language—Grammar—1950–   2. English language—Rhetoric.
I. Wood, Merle W.   II. Title.
PE1112.H56 1991
428.2—dc20   91-26864
                                          CIP

1 2 3 4 5 6 7 8 9 0 H 98 97 96 95 94 93 92

Printed in the United States of America

 This book is printed on recycled, acid-free paper that meets Environmental
Protection Agency standards.

PREFACE

Basic skills are required for each of us to conduct our personal and business dealings. Increasing numbers of adults need to acquire these basic skills so they can improve both their personal interactions and employment opportunities.

As a result, the LIFE Series was developed because South-Western believes that **L**earning **I**s **F**or **E**veryone (**LIFE**). The LIFE Series provides adults with the basic skills they need to succeed in their personal lives and on the job.

THE LIFE SERIES

The LIFE Series is a self-paced, competency-based program specifically designed to enable adults to develop basic skills for job and personal use. Each book in the series provides interesting material, realistic examples, practical applications, and flexible instruction to promote learner success and self-confidence.

The LIFE Series is divided into three basic skill areas—communication skills, math skills, and life skills. *Grammar and Writing for Job and Personal Use* is one of the communication skills books in the LIFE Series. Each text-workbook is complete and may be used individually or in a series. The following is a complete list of LIFE Series titles.

Communication Skills

> *Spelling for Job and Personal Use*
> *Reading for Job and Personal Use*
> *Grammar and Writing for Job and Personal Use*
> *Punctuation, Capitalization, and Handwriting for Job and Personal Use*
> *Listening and Speaking for Job and Personal Use*

Math Skills

> *Basic Math for Job and Personal Use*
> *Decimals, Fractions, and Percentages for Job and Personal Use*
> *Calculator Math for Job and Personal Use*

Life Skills

Career Planning and Development
Problem Solving and Decision Making
Self-Esteem and Getting Ahead
Money Management
Finding and Holding a Job

STRUCTURE AND ORGANIZATION

Each book in the LIFE Series has the same appearance and structure, enabling learners to experience more success and gain self-confidence as they progress. Competency-based instruction is also used throughout. Clear objectives are presented first, followed by short segments of material with specific exercises for immediate reinforcement.

The organization of *Grammar and Writing for Job and Personal Use* reflects the development of basic grammar and writing skills and the applications of these skills to employment and personal use. Part One, Understanding Basic English Grammar, provides the foundation needed to write correctly. In Part Two, Developing Your Writing Skills, students will apply the basic rules learned in Part One by creating sentences, paragraphs, notes, and messages. The writing activities in Part Three, Writing to Get a Job, prepare students to complete documents needed to get a job. They will prepare a personal profile, a resume, and learn to complete a job application. Part Four, Writing on the Job, provides opportunities to complete forms and write memos and business letters—the most commonly written documents in the workplace. In Part Five, Writing for Personal Use, students develop a self-improvement action plan by thinking about future goals they want to achieve.

The Glossary, Index, Answers, and Personal Progress Record at the end of *Grammar and Writing for Job and Personal Use* are designed to facilitate and enhance independent student learning and achievement.

SPECIAL FEATURES OF GRAMMAR AND WRITING FOR JOB AND PERSONAL USE

Grammar and Writing for Job and Personal Use is a complete and comprehensive package. It provides the student with learning material written specifically to meet the unique needs of the adult learner and the instructor with support materials to facilitate student success. Some special features include the following:

Design Characteristics. Each text-workbook in the LIFE Series, including *Grammar and Writing for Job and Personal Use,* uses a larger typeface to make it easier for the student to use and to read.

Appropriate Content. Real-life issues and skills are emphasized throughout the text, with relevant examples and illustrations provided to which the student can relate.

Objectives. Instructional objectives are clearly stated for each unit, letting students know what they will learn.

Checkpoints. Checkpoints follow short segments of instruction and provide students with an opportunity to immediately use what they have just learned.

Goals. Goals are listed for each exercise to give the student motivation and direction.

Study Breaks. Each unit contains study breaks that provide a refreshing break from study while contributing to the global literacy goal of the student.

Summaries. A summary of the student's accomplishments is provided at the end of each unit providing encouragement and reinforcement.

Putting It Together. The end-of-unit activities cover the theory presented in the Checkpoints and provide goals for students to measure their own skill development and success.

Glossary. Important terms in the text are printed in bold and defined the first time they are used. These terms are listed and defined in the Glossary for easy reference.

Answers. Answers for all the Checkpoints and Activities are provided at the back of the text-workbook and designed for easy reference to facilitate independent and self-paced learning.

Personal Progress Record. Students keep track of their own progress by recording scores on a Personal Progress Record. Students can measure their own success by comparing their scores to evaluation guides provided for each unit. Whenever a student's total score for a unit is below the minimum requirement, the student may request a Bonus Exercise from the instructor.

SPECIAL FEATURES OF
THE INSTRUCTOR'S MANUAL ━━━━━

The Instructor's Manual provides general instructional strategies and specific teaching suggestions for *Grammar and Writing for Job and Personal Use*, along with supplementary bonus exercises and answers, testing materials, and a Certificate of Completion.

Bonus Exercises. Second-chance exercises for all activities are offered through bonus exercises provided in the Instructor's Manual. These bonus exercises enable instructors to provide additional applications to those students whose scores do not meet the desired achievement level for a unit. Answers to all bonus exercises are also provided and can be duplicated for student use.

Testing Materials. Four assessment tools, entitled "Checking What You Know," are provided. These tests may be used interchangeably as pre-tests or post-tests allowing for flexible use.

Certificate of Completion. Upon completion of *Grammar and Writing for Job and Personal Use,* a student's success is recognized through a Certificate of Completion. This certificate has a listing of topics that were covered in the text. A master certificate is included in the Instructor's Manual.

Grammar and Writing for Job and Personal Use is designed specifically to help you invest in your adult learners' futures and to meet your instructional needs.

Special thanks to Anita Brownstein of Drake Business Schools in New York City for her helpful comments and suggestions on this text.

CONTENTS

GETTING ACQUAINTED

Writing is a necessary method of communication. It is one of the ways you can express your thoughts and feelings. The appearance of a written document creates a lasting impression on the reader. Using correct grammar, capitalization, and punctuation will help achieve a positive reaction.

In the workplace, writing includes

- taking telephone messages,
- completing forms,
- creating letters and memos, and
- giving instructions.

In looking for a job, writing includes

- preparing resumes,
- filling out job applications,
- answering want ads, and
- creating follow-up letters.

Personal writing includes

- preparing shopping lists,
- writing notes and messages,
- creating letters, and
- keeping records.

Being able to communicate clearly in writing can make an employee more valuable to an employer. It will also be an advantage to have this skill in everyday living.

You may be taking this program to improve or review your grammar and writing skills. If English is not your native language, you may be taking this program to develop better grammar and writing skills. Regardless of the reason, *Grammar and Writing for Job and Personal Use* should help you improve your basic grammar and writing skills for employment and personal use.

HOW YOU WILL LEARN ━━━━━━━━━━

The system used in this book will help you learn. You need to know how this system works.

Learn at Your Own Pace

You will progress through the lessons in *Grammar and Writing for Job and Personal Use* while working at your own pace. Don't be concerned that you may move faster, or slower, than other students. You are to work at *your* best pace and speed.

Learn Skills Successfully

Learning objectives before each lesson will let you know what you are to accomplish. In each lesson, you will study a topic. In most instances, examples are provided to help you. When you have shown that you know the topic, you will move on to the next one. It will be possible to review how well you have learned the topic by completing the Checkpoints and Activities features in each lesson. If you have not learned the topic, you must study harder on that section. By this method, you can be sure of how well you are doing as you move through each step in this book.

Check Your Own Success

It is up to you to keep track of your own success. After most of the activities in the book, you should check your work by looking up the answers in the back of the book. After checking your work, record your score on your Personal Progress Record, which is also at the back of the book.

WHAT YOU WILL LEARN ━━━━━━━━━━

As you study *Grammar and Writing for Job and Personal Use,* you will learn the basic English grammar skills needed in writing. You will apply these skills to writing situations common in the workplace and in your personal life. As your skills improve, you will see how writing can help you clarify your thinking, organize your thoughts, and explore how you feel. You will discover that writing can be an exciting process.

To achieve the objectives of this book, you will study the following five parts:

Part One   Understanding Basic English Grammar
Part Two   Developing Your Writing Skills

Part Three   Writing to Get a Job
Part Four   Writing on the Job
Part Five   Writing for Personal Use

Understanding Basic English Grammar

There are certain basic rules to follow in writing. Part One provides the foundation for writing correctly, including the correct use of words in sentences, and the rules for capitalization and punctuation.

Developing Your Writing Skills

Writing is a building process. In Part Two you will apply the basic rules learned in Part One by creating sentences, paragraphs, notes, and messages. As you develop your skills, you will feel more confident about your writing ability.

Writing to Get a Job

Part Three covers writing about yourself and your background. You will prepare a personal profile and a resume, and learn to complete a job application. You will also learn the proper format for writing personal and business letters. The writing activities in this part prepare you for completing documents needed to get a job.

Writing on the Job

Most occupations require some writing. Part Four provides you with activities in which you will write forms, memos, and business letters. These are the most commonly written documents in the workplace. In addition, you will learn the importance of following the instructions on various forms.

Writing for Personal Use

In Part Five, you have an opportunity to use your writing skills in a different way. You will develop a self-improvement action plan by writing goals for your future. The exercises will also give you a chance to develop your talent for creative expression.

All students will be expected to do Parts Three, Four, and Five of *Grammar and Writing for Job and Personal Use*. Some students may not need to complete Parts One and Two. Your instructor will help you determine the part at which you will begin.

SPECIAL FEATURES ▬▬▬▬▬▬▬▬

Grammar and Writing for Job and Personal Use has a number of special features. These features will help you learn and apply the material successfully.

Glossary

Key words and terms are always in **bold type** when they are defined. The key words and terms appear in the Glosssary in alphabetical order at the back of the book.

Breaks from Instruction

Throughout the book, breaks are provided to expand your understanding of the use of language. These are presented under the headings of *Evolution of Writing, Writing Gems,* and *Getting Ready to Go to Work.*

Checkpoints

Exercises called Checkpoints are frequently provided for you to check your understanding of a topic. You must meet the desired achievement goal before moving on to the next topic.

Putting It Together

At the end of each unit is a section called Putting It Together. This section has one or more Activities, which are similar to the Checkpoints. These Activities will help you apply the skills you have learned in the unit.

Margin Notes

The margin notes state the desired achievement goal for each Checkpoint and Activity. The goal should be met before continuing with the rest of the unit.

Bonus Checkpoints and Bonus Activities

You may not reach the desired goal on every Checkpoint or Activity. When this happens, you must read the lesson again and then complete a Bonus Checkpoint or Bonus Activity. These Bonus features cover the same information presented in the unit, and provide you with a second chance to succeed. Your instructor will supply the Bonus Checkpoints and Bonus Activities. Your instructor also has the answer key to these exercises, which you will use to check your work. When you score higher on a bonus exercise than you did on the original exercise, you may change your score on your Personal Progress Record.

Answers

Answers to all the Checkpoints and Activities are provided at the back of the book. There is a color bar along the edges of the answer pages that makes them easy to find. Use these pages to check your work. Always do the Checkpoints and Activities *before* you look at the answers. Use the answers as a tool to check your work—not as a means of completing the exercises.

Personal Progress Record

After checking your work, record your score on your Personal Progress Record. This form also is located at the back of the book. After you complete a unit, you will be able to determine your level of success.

Certificate of Completion

When you finish *Grammar and Writing for Job and Personal Use,* you may be eligible for a Certificate of Completion. Your instructor will explain the skill level required for you to earn this award.

READY TO START

You are now ready to start improving your grammar and writing skills. As you study these units, think of how the skills you are learning can help you in a job or in your personal life. With study and practice, you will learn ways of using the language to present your thoughts easily and directly. Thus, the written language will always be a valuable and effective tool for you to use in communicating with others.

PART ONE
UNDERSTANDING BASIC ENGLISH GRAMMAR

UNIT 1
**THE SENTENCE
AND ITS PARTS**

UNIT 2
PARTS OF SPEECH

UNIT 3
CAPITALIZATION

UNIT 4
PUNCTUATION

1

UNIT 1
THE SENTENCE AND ITS PARTS

WHAT YOU WILL LEARN

When you finish this unit, you will be able to:
- Define a sentence.
- Identify the subject in a sentence.
- Identify the predicate in a sentence.
- Identify the subject in a sentence that asks a question.

WHAT IS A SENTENCE?

A **sentence** is one or more words that give a complete idea. It may make a statement. A sentence may ask a question or tell someone to do something. It may also express a strong feeling. All sentences have two basic parts—these are called the subject and the predicate.

THE SUBJECT

The **subject** tells *who* or *what* is doing something. The subject tells you *who* or *what* is being described.

✔ CHECKPOINT 1-1

YOUR GOAL:
Get 4 or more answers correct.

Choose the word or words from the following list that best completes each sentence. Write the words in the spaces provided. The first one is completed as an example.

The child	The President
Dr. Fung	O. J. Simpson
Los Angeles	The original painting

● _____Los Angeles_____ is a big city.

1. _____ was a football player.

2. _____ was expensive.

3. _____ goes to nursery school.

4. _____ is a dentist.

5. _____ lives in Washington, D.C.

☞ *Check your work. Record your score.*

YOU HAVE JUST WRITTEN COMPLETE SENTENCES. THE WORDS YOU CHOSE FOR EACH SENTENCE ARE CALLED THE **SUBJECT** OF THE SENTENCE. EACH SENTENCE GIVES A COMPLETE IDEA. REFER TO ILLUSTRATION 1-1 FOR AN EASY WAY TO REMEMBER HOW TO FIND THE SUBJECT.

Illustration 1-1

Finding the
Subject

REMEMBER—TO FIND THE SUBJECT . . .

ask **WHO** or **WHAT** is doing something

OR

ask **WHO** or **WHAT** is being described.

✔ *CHECKPOINT 1-2*

YOUR GOAL:
Get 4 or more
answers correct.

Answer the questions following each sentence. Write the subject of each sentence in the space provided. The first one is completed as an example.

● Los Angeles is a big city.

   What city is a big city?   Los Angeles _____

1. O. J. Simpson was a football player.

   Who was a football player?   _____

2. The original painting was expensive.

   What was expensive?   _____

3. The child goes to nursery school.

   Who goes to nursery school?   _____

4. Dr. Fung is a dentist.

   Who is a dentist?   _____

5. The President lives in Washington, D.C.

   Who lives in Washington, D.C.?   _____

☞ *Check your work. Record your score.*

The Simple Subject

The *simple subject* is the key word in the subject. The key word or words tell *who* or *what* the sentence is about. The simple subject is the person, place, or thing the sentence is talking about or doing the action.

Example of a Simple Subject:

Steve's new gray car is a four-door sedan.
(*Steve's new gray car* is the subject. The simple subject or key word is *car.* The words *Steve's, new,* and *gray* tell you about the car. They describe the car. These words are called *modifiers.* A **modifier** tells you more about another word.)

In some cases, the simple subject may have more than one word. For example, a person's first and last names could be the simple subject. A state name with two words could be the simple subject.

Examples of Simple Subjects with Two Words:

John Lennon sang with the Beatles.
North Carolina is a beautiful state.
(*John Lennon* and *North Carolina* are simple subjects. John Lennon is *who* is being described in the sentence. North Carolina is *what* is being described in the sentence.)

EVOLUTION OF WRITING—The Invention of Paper

Can you imagine writing without paper? The Chinese invented paper in 105 A.D. They also printed the first text. They carved images on wood blocks and then applied ink to the blocks. Paper was then pressed on the blocks to transfer the images.

The Compound Subject

A *compound subject* is made up of two or more simple subjects. Usually, the word *and* will connect the simple subjects.

Examples of Compound Subjects:

Students and teachers work together.
(*Students* and *teachers* are simple subjects. Students and teachers are *who* is being described in the sentence.)

Birds, cats, and dogs are in the pet store.
(*Birds, cats,* and *dogs* are simple subjects. Birds, cats, and dogs are *what* is being described in the sentence.)

CHECKPOINT 1-3

YOUR GOAL:
Get 4 or more answers correct.

Underline the simple subject in each of the following sentences. The first one is completed as an example.

- <u>Anthony McKay</u> went on a job interview today.

1. Lenora and Bill have three children.

2. Mei Ching lived in Hong Kong.

3. Computers and copiers are used in offices.

4. Walking is good exercise.

5. David Taylor works as an aircraft engineer.

☞ **Check your work. Record your score.**

THE PREDICATE

The **predicate** tells about the subject. The predicate can show action. It can tell what the subject *does* or *did* or is *doing*. The predicate can describe the subject. It can tell what the subject *is* or *was*.

CHECKPOINT 1-4

YOUR GOAL:
Get 4 or more answers correct.

Choose the predicate from the following list that best completes each sentence. Write the words in the spaces provided. The first one is completed as an example.

is a problem for the environment
are replacing records
was a civil rights leader
is a computer service technician
is common among adults
exercise daily

● Angela _____ is a computer service technician _____.

1. Pamela and Terry _____.

2. Heart disease _____.

3. Dr. Martin Luther King, Jr., _____.

4. Compact discs _____.

5. Pollution _____.

☞ *Check your work. Record your score.*

YOU HAVE JUST WRITTEN COMPLETE SENTENCES.
THE WORDS YOU CHOSE FOR EACH SENTENCE ARE
CALLED THE **PREDICATE** OF THE SENTENCE. EACH
SENTENCE GIVES A COMPLETE IDEA.

CHECKPOINT 1-5

YOUR GOAL:
Get 4 or more
answers correct.

Write the predicate for each of the following sentences in the
space provided. The first one is completed as an example.

● Angela is a computer service technician.

What **is** Angela? _____ is a computer service technician _____.

1. Pamela and Terry exercise daily.

What **do** Pamela and Terry do? _____.

2. Heart disease is common among adults.

What **is** heart disease? _____.

3. Dr. Martin Luther King, Jr., was a civil rights leader.

Who **was** Dr. Martin Luther King, Jr.? _____.

4. Compact discs are replacing records.

    What **are** compact discs doing? _____.

5. Pollution is a problem for the environment.

    What **is** pollution a problem for? _____.

☞ *Check your work. Record your score.*

EVOLUTION OF WRITING—The First Paper

What was paper first made from? The first paper was made from treebark, hemp waste, old rags, and fish nets. The art of papermaking reached Europe in the twelfth century. The Chinese invented papermaking 1,000 years before. Today, paper is made from wood pulp.

The Simple Predicate

The *simple predicate* is the key word in the predicate. A simple predicate tells what the subject *does* or *did*. A simple predicate can also tell what the subject *is* or *was*.

Examples of Simple Predicates:

Eric eats strawberries.
(The simple predicate is *eats*.)

Eric imagined strawberries with whipped cream.
(The simple predicate is *imagined*.)

The Compound Predicate

A *compound predicate* is made up of two or more simple predicates. Usually, the word *and* will connect the simple predicates.

Example of a Compound Predicate:

Eric eats strawberries and drinks milk.
(*Eats* and *drinks* are simple predicates used together to create a compound predicate. They describe what the subject *does*.)

CHECKPOINT 1-6

YOUR GOAL:
Get 4 or more
answers correct.

Underline the simple predicate in each of the following sentences. The first one is completed as an example.

- The salesperson <u>worked</u> in the evening.

1. Carlotta plays racquetball and volleyball.

2. She sang and danced beautifully.

3. The dog barked all night long.

4. Joanne moved from California to Oregon.

5. Don and Barbara collect antique furniture.

☞ *Check your work. Record your score.*

SENTENCES THAT ASK QUESTIONS

There are other types of sentences. Some sentences ask questions. They ask about the subject. See Illustration 1-2 for questions asked about the subject.

Illustration 1-2

Sentences
That Ask
Questions

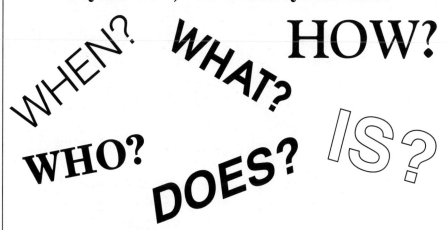

TO FIND THE SUBJECT IN A SENTENCE THAT ASKS

A QUESTION, ASK THESE QUESTIONS:

WHEN?   WHAT?   HOW?

WHO?   DOES?   IS?

Example of a Sentence That Asks a Question:

Is she looking for a job?

Here are two ways to find the subject of a sentence that asks a question.

1. Change the words around to make the sentence tell something.

    She is looking for a job.

2. Ask **who** or **what** the sentence is about.
    She is **who** the sentence is about.

The subject of the sentence is *she*.

CHECKPOINT 1-7

YOUR GOAL:
Get 4 or more answers correct.

Underline the simple subject in each of the following sentences. The first one is completed as an example.

● Does <u>Carolyn</u> have a ride to work?

1. Have you completed the job application?

2. Does he know the keyboard?

3. When will Hideo be arriving?

4. Would you like fish or chicken?

5. Is the apartment ready for painting?

☞ *Check your work. Record your score.*

WHAT YOU HAVE LEARNED

As a result of completing this unit, you have learned that:
● A sentence is one or more words that give a complete thought.
● The subject tells who or what is doing something or being described.
● The predicate tells about the subject.
● The subject in a sentence that asks a question can be found by asking questions.

PUTTING IT TOGETHER

ACTIVITY 1-1 **YOUR GOAL:** Get 8 or more answers correct.

Underline the subject once and the predicate twice in each of the following sentences. The first one is completed as an example.

- The <u>firefighters</u> <u><u>rushed to the accident</u></u>.

1. Virginia and John traveled to San Antonio by train.

2. Part-time jobs are available at the department store.

3. What is your favorite food?

4. Doug and Valerie saved to buy a home.

5. Karen dressed properly for the job interview.

6. Her parents were caring and encouraging.

7. The computer software requires a hard disk.

8. Pablo worked in advertising and construction.

9. The restaurant serves Cambodian food.

10. Mark attends junior high school.

☞ *Check your work. Record your score.*

ACTIVITY 1-2 **YOUR GOAL:** Get 8 or more answers correct.

Using the sentences from Activity 1-1, underline the simple subject once. Underline the simple predicate twice. Compound subjects and compound predicates may also be found in the sentences. The first one is completed as an example.

- The <u>firefighters</u> <u><u>rushed</u></u> to the accident.

1. Virginia and John traveled to San Antonio by train.

2. Part-time jobs are available at the department store.

3. What is your favorite food?

4. Doug and Valerie saved to buy a home.

5. Karen dressed properly for the job interview.

6. Her parents were caring and encouraging.

7. The computer software requires a hard disk.

8. Pablo worked in advertising and construction.

9. The restaurant serves Cambodian food.

10. Mark attends junior high school.

☞ *Check your work. Record your score.*

ACTIVITY 1-3   YOUR GOAL: Get 8 or more answers correct.

Read the paragraph. Then read the list of words following the paragraph. Complete each sentence by selecting one simple subject or simple predicate from the list. Use each word only once. As you use each word, place a check mark beside it. Write the word in the space provided. The first two are completed as an example.

Miguel Ruiz ____attends____ a vocational school. He ____is____ learning to be an electronics technician. He _____ to finish the two-year program in June. His _____, Miss Yee, is proud of his progress. _____ will _____ a Certificate of Completion at the end of his training. Miguel also _____ while going to school. He is a Nurse Assistant at Piner's Nursing Center. At the convalescent home, he _____ and bathes patients. He _____ his patients, and they like him. On weekends, Miguel _____ soccer with his two daughters. He _____ his son's baseball team. Miguel and his wife, _____, volunteer to work at their daughter's day-care center. Miguel Ruiz is a hardworking and ambitious man.

feeds	likes	Consuelo
plays	instructor	✓ is
✓ attends	Miguel	coaches
plans	receive	works

☞ *Check your work. Record your score.*

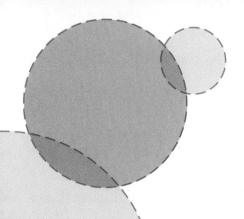

UNIT 2
PARTS OF SPEECH

WHAT YOU WILL LEARN

When you finish this unit, you will be able to:
- Understand how words are used in sentences.
- Identify the eight parts of speech.
- Write sentences using the parts of speech.

WORDS USED IN SENTENCES

Good communication skills are required in most jobs. These skills include the ability to speak, listen, and write. To express yourself in writing, you have to decide which words to use. Understanding the different parts of speech will help you put your thoughts and words into sentences.

THE EIGHT PARTS OF SPEECH

Parts of speech refers to how words are used in sentences. Words can be used in eight different ways. The eight parts of speech are noun, pronoun, verb, adjective, adverb, preposition, conjunction, and interjection.

Nouns

A **noun** is a word that names a person, place, thing, or idea. An idea also includes feelings. Nouns include these words: *Uncle Herb, mother, brother, soccer, highway, bridge, Texas, carburetor, television, birthday, Memorial Day.*

Examples of Nouns:

Susan drives to work.
(*Susan* is a noun. Susan is the name of a *person*.)

He lives in Florida.
(*Florida* is a noun. Florida is the name of a *place*.)

The car has been driven 65,000 miles.
(*Car* is a noun. A car is a *thing.*)

It is always best to tell the truth.
(*Truth* is a noun. Truth is an *idea.*)

Common Nouns

A *common noun* is one that does not name a particular person, place, thing, or idea. Common nouns are not capitalized. Common nouns shown in Illustration 2-1 include a telephone, pen, paper, stamps, and an envelope.

Illustration 2-1

Common
Nouns

EVOLUTION OF WRITING—Early Writing Material

In 3100 B.C., the Egyptians developed a new writing material called *papyrus.* This durable paper was made from stalks of the papyrus plant. Strips of the stalk were pressed and beaten into sheets. They were then smoothed together with rocks or shells.

Proper Nouns

A *proper noun* is the name of a specific person, place, or thing. The first letter of a proper noun is capitalized. If the proper noun has two words, the first letter in each word is capitalized. Proper nouns shown in Illustration 2-2 include the Statue of Liberty and the Eiffel Tower.

Illustration 2-2

Proper
Nouns

CHECKPOINT 2-1

YOUR GOAL:
Get 14 or more answers correct.

Decide whether each noun from the following list is a person, place, thing, or idea. Write the nouns under each heading in the space provided. The first one under each column is completed as an example.

tractor	South America	freedom
butcher	joy	restaurant
child	love	Grand Canyon
office	manager	food
newspaper	Ms. Guiterrez	drafter
Boston	September	stress
telephone	self-confidence	

Person	Place	Thing	Idea
butcher	South America	tractor	freedom

☞ *Check your work. Record your score.*

YOUR GOAL:
Write 12 nouns. Get 12 points.

Now write your own nouns. Write three nouns under each heading in the space provided.

Person	Place	Thing	Idea

☞ *Review your answers with a classmate. Record your score.*

Pronouns

A **pronoun** is a word used in place of a noun. Pronouns include the following words: *I, you, he, she, it, we, they, myself, themselves, herself, one another.* Pronouns may be singular or plural.

Singular Pronouns

A *singular pronoun* refers to one person, place, or thing.

Examples of Singular Pronouns:

Emily likes cats.
She likes cats.
(*She* is used in place of *Emily.*)

Glen will attend the graduation.
He will attend the graduation.
(*He* is used in place of *Glen.*)

The truck has four-wheel drive.
It has four-wheel drive.
(*It* is used in place of *truck.*)

Plural Pronouns

A *plural pronoun* refers to more than one person, place, or thing.

Examples of Plural Pronouns:

Antonio and I are going bowling.
We are going bowling.
(*We* is used in place of *Antonio and I.*)

Marcia and Bruce went to the Super Bowl.
They went to the Super Bowl.
(*They* is used in place of *Marcia and Bruce.*)

The following lists show singular and plural pronouns. *You* can mean either one or more than one. Review them before completing Checkpoint 2-2.

Singular: I, you, he, she, it, me
Plural: we, you, they

CHECKPOINT 2-2

YOUR GOAL:
Get 4 or more
answers correct.

Write the pronoun for each of the following sentences in the space provided. The first one is completed as an example.

● Cameron is on a low-cholesterol diet.

_____He_____ is on a low-cholesterol diet.

1. Mr. and Mrs. Perez are taking a cruise to Hawaii.

   _____ are taking a cruise to Hawaii.

2. July and August are warm months.

   _____ are warm months.

3. The copier needs to be repaired.

   _____ needs to be repaired.

4. Chi-liang, the waiter, is from Shanghai.

   _____ is from Shanghai.

5. Ms. Fitzgerald and I visited the culinary school.

   _____ visited the culinary school.

☞ *Check your work. Record your score.*

Verbs

A **verb** is a word that expresses an action. It is an action you can see or an action you cannot see. A verb is also a state of being. Verbs include these words: *is, were, jogs, ate, painted, has, write, dancing, worked, laughs, singing, enjoys, wants.*

Examples of Verbs:
Victor was *talking* to his supervisor.
(*Talking* expresses an action you can see.)

I *enjoy* gardening.
(*Enjoy* expresses an action you cannot see.)

They *were* tired.
(*Were* is a state of being.)

Linking Verbs

As stated before, some verbs express a state of being. These verbs are called *linking verbs*. They do not refer to an action. A linking verb often connects the subject with a predicate or adjective. The most common linking verbs are *is, are, was, were, been, am*.

Examples of Linking Verbs:

He *is* a competent secretary.
The home *was* located in the country.

CHECKPOINT 2-3

YOUR GOAL:
Get 4 or more answers correct.

Underline the verb in each of the following sentences. The first one is completed as an example.

● Raul <u>worked</u> in the auto detailing department.

1. Leilani trains show horses.

2. The mail carrier delivered the package.

3. She danced at the party.

4. Ben yelled for help.

5. The instructor is demonstrating the machine.

☞ *Check your work. Record your score.*

Present and Past Tense Verbs

The spelling of verbs indicates when the action took place. *Tense* means *time*. *Present tense verbs* show action taking place now. *Past tense verbs* show that the action has already taken place.

Examples of Verb Tenses:

I *ask* my mother to baby-sit. (present)
I *asked* my mother to baby-sit. (past)

The bus *stops* on Main Street. (present)
The bus *stopped* on Main Street. (past)

Melinda *drives* to work. (present)
Melinda *drove* to work. (past)

EVOLUTION OF WRITING—Early Writing Material

Ancient Greeks and Romans made books from blocks of wood. The blocks were coated with wax or plaster. A stylus, usually made from metal or bone, was used for writing. After the books were completed, all the pieces of wood were tied together with rope or leather.

Regular Verbs

A *regular verb* is a verb that becomes past tense by adding *d* or *ed* to the present tense. Study the lists of present and past tense verbs.

Present: talk, ask, walk, jump, improve, learn
Past: talked, asked, walked, jumped, improved, learned

In some words with one syllable, such as *stop* and *tag,* the consonant is doubled before *ed* is added. Consonants and vowels are defined in Illustration 2-3.

Illustration 2-3

Vowels and Consonants

> **VOWELS** are *a, e, i, o, u,* and sometimes *y.* All the
>
> other letters in the alphabet are **CONSONANTS**.

Study the following lists of one-syllable words. Present and past tenses are shown.

Present: stop, drop, step, tag, nap, chip
Past: stopped, dropped, stepped, tagged, napped, chipped

With most verbs that end with a *y,* the *y* is changed to an *i* and *ed* is added. Study the following lists of present and past tense verbs.

Present: try, cry, study, deny, spy, apply
Past: tried, cried, studied, denied, spied, applied

CHECKPOINT 2-4

YOUR GOAL:
Get 5 or more answers correct.

Write the past tense for each of the following verbs in the space provided. The first two are completed as examples.

● thank ___thanked___   ● hop ___hopped___

1. live _____   2. drag _____

3. fry _____   4. praise _____

5. owe _____   6. hire _____

☞ *Check your work. Record your score.*

Irregular Verbs

An *irregular verb* forms its past tense by changing the word in ways other than by adding *d* or *ed*. Some irregular verbs are spelled the same in present and past tense. The following lists show some irregular verbs. Appendix A includes a more complete list of irregular verbs.

Present	Past	Present	Past
am	was	have	had
burst	burst	buy	bought
draw	drew	ride	rode
drink	drank	say	said
drive	drove	speak	spoke
eat	ate	tell	told
go	went	write	wrote

Adjectives

An **adjective** is a word used to describe a noun or pronoun. Adjectives include these words: *a, an, the, wonderful, beautiful, young, healthy, friendly.*

Examples of Adjectives:

The *friendly* woman works.
He likes *spicy* food.

CHECKPOINT 2-5

YOUR GOAL:
Get 8 or more answers correct.

Underline the adjectives in the following list. The first two are completed as examples.

- <u>beautiful</u> clothes
- <u>cheerful</u> salesperson

1. ancient dinosaurs
2. deadly disease
3. positive attitude
4. happy childhood
5. generous parents
6. cold weather
7. patient nurse
8. new car
9. hardworking person
10. skilled electrician

☞ *Check your work. Record your score.*

The most frequently used adjectives are *a, an,* and *the.* These words are called *articles. A* and *an* are called *indefinite articles.* They do not point out a particular person, place, thing, or idea. *The* is called a *definite article.* It always points out a particular person, place, thing, or idea.

Examples of Articles:

The explosion made *a* loud sound.
A good breakfast was recommended by *the* doctor.

Adverbs

An **adverb** is a word used to tell more about a verb, adjective, or another adverb. An adverb tells how, when, where, or to what extent or degree. Adverbs often end in *ly* because *ly* added to an adjective makes an adverb. Adverbs include these words: *weekly, faster, well, noisy, happily.*

Examples of Adverbs:

Pilar cheered *enthusiastically.*   (how?)
The mail arrived *late.*   (when?)
Frank Soo Hoo lived *there.*   (where?)
The movie was *very* exciting.   (to what extent or degree?)

CHECKPOINT 2-6

YOUR GOAL:
Get 4 or more
answers correct.

Underline the adverb in each of the following sentences. The first one is completed as an example.

- We waited <u>patiently</u> for the results.

1. Minnie sews beautifully.

2. The truck drivers drove slowly on the icy road.

3. Arthur carefully read the contract.

4. The application was completed legibly.

5. We are leaving for Mexico tomorrow.

☞ *Check your work. Record your score.*

Prepositions

A **preposition** is a word or group of words that shows how two words or ideas are related to each other. An easy way to remember prepositions is shown in Illustration 2-4. Prepositions include these words: *about, after, around, at, before, but, for, from, in, of, on, since, to,* and *with.* A more complete list of prepositions is in Appendix B.

Examples of Prepositions:

He hasn't worked *since* his accident.
My sister was born *on* Cinco de Mayo.

Illustration 2-4

Prepositions

PREPOSITIONS—One way to remember them is to imagine a bee flying around a hive. Whatever the bee can do to show its relationship to the hive is a PREPOSITION.

A BEE CAN FLY
under the hive,
above the hive,
around the hive,
inside the hive,
past the hive.

✔ CHECKPOINT 2-7

YOUR GOAL:
Get 4 or more answers correct.

Write the prepositions for each of the following sentences in the space provided. The first one is completed as an example.

● _____after_____   We will meet after the ball game.

1. _____   The fire fighter was trapped under the house.

2. _____   Patrick walked the dog down the street.

3. _____   We will be driving over the Bay Bridge.

4. _____   The bank will be closed during the holiday.

5. _____   Lola received a letter from her daughter.

☞ *Check your work. Record your score.*

Conjunctions

A **conjunction** connects individual words or groups of words. Common conjunctions are: *and, but, for, nor, or, so, yet.*

Examples of Conjunctions:

Evelyn *and* Desmond enjoy traveling.
Next year they will visit Europe *and* China.
They will take their son *or* daughter with them.
They wanted to take a cruise *but* decided to fly.

✔ CHECKPOINT 2-8

YOUR GOAL:
Get 4 or more answers correct.

Underline the conjunction in each of the following sentences. The first one is completed as an example.

● The game was canceled due to wind <u>and</u> rain.

1. Billie Jean King and Chris Evert are tennis players.

2. The painters worked swiftly yet carefully.

3. He will learn to play the guitar or piano.

4. The job is difficult but enjoyable.

5. I arrived early for a front-row seat.

☞ *Check your work. Record your score.*

Interjections

An **interjection** is a word or words used to express strong emotion or surprise. Interjections include these words: *help, oh, wow, whew, yippee.* An exclamation mark (!) often follows an interjection.

Examples of Interjections:

Wow! I don't believe I won.
Whew! I am exhausted.

✔ CHECKPOINT 2-9

YOUR GOAL:
Get 4 or more
answers correct.

Underline the interjection in each of the following sentences. The first one is completed as an example.

● <u>Incredible!</u> A hole in one.

1. Oh, no! I have a flat tire.

2. Stop! The light is red.

3. Hooray! I finished the race.

4. Ouch! That stings.

5. Wonderful! She got all A's.

☞ *Check your work. Record your score.*

WHAT YOU HAVE LEARNED

As a result of completing this unit, you have learned to:
● Use words in sentences.
● Identify the eight parts of speech.
● Use the parts of speech in sentences.

PUTTING IT TOGETHER

ACTIVITY 2-1   **YOUR GOAL:** Get 5 or more answers correct.

Write the letter that describes how each of the following parts of speech is used in the space provided. The first one is completed as an example.

- ● _____h_____ Conjunctions
- 1. _____ Pronouns
- 2. _____ Adjectives
- 3. _____ Interjections
- 4. _____ Prepositions
- 5. _____ Adverbs
- 6. _____ Nouns
- 7. _____ Verbs

a. usually express action.

b. express strong emotion.

c. name a person, place, thing, or idea.

d. tell more about a verb, adjective, or adverb.

e. are used in place of nouns.

f. describe nouns or pronouns.

g. show the relationship of words or ideas to each other.

h. connect words.

☞ *Check your work. Record your score.*

ACTIVITY 2-2   **YOUR GOAL:** Get 32 or more answers correct.

Underline the part of speech you are asked to identify in each section. Some sentences may have more than one noun, pronoun, verb, or other part of speech. The first one in each section is completed as an example.

Nouns ● <u>Colors</u> of the <u>flag</u> are red, white, and blue.

1. George Washington Carver made the peanut famous.

2. The highway was damaged during the earthquake.

3. Holidays are fun, but weekends are better.

Pronouns ● <u>He</u> left the light on, and <u>she</u> turned <u>it</u> off.

4. It was a sad day when they parted.

5. You may be right, but I think you are wrong.

6. She added the dinner check to see if it was right.

Verbs ● Things <u>were</u> different when we <u>were</u> young.

7. Where on earth are they?

8. They worked hard, but played harder.

9. Write me a poem, and sing me a song.

Adjectives ● The sunset was a <u>bright</u> orange.

10. They enjoyed their summer vacation.

11. She likes warm weather.

12. His yellow cotton shirt was wrinkled.

Adverbs ● The nurse <u>carefully</u> moved the patient.

13. He attended class weekly.

14. The mechanic quickly changed the tire.

15. The rock band played loudly.

Prepositions ● It was a movie <u>about</u> the Vietnam War.

16. He rode to work on a bicycle.

17. Please let me go with you.

18. The tractor was beyond repair.

Conjunctions ● You were here, <u>and</u> I was there.

19. I forgot, or I would have told you.

20. She is learning reading, writing, and math.

21. It may be hard, but you will learn.

Interjections ● <u>Wow!</u> That was wonderful.

22. Hooray! We made it.

23. Step on it! I don't want to be late.

24. Oh, no! I broke it.

25. Ouch! My cut hurts.

☞ *Check your work. Record your score.*

ACTIVITY 2-3   YOUR GOAL: Write 16 sentences. Get 16 points.

There are six words listed after each part of speech. Pick two words and write two sentences using these words in the space provided. The first one is completed as an example.

Nouns   wife   school   husband
                car   church   television

● _____ My husband is a very kind man _____.

1. _____.

2. _____.

Pronouns   me   she   we
                he   they   myself

3. _____.

4. _____.

Verbs   ate   dancing   painted
                went   were   laughed

5. _____.

6. _____.

Adjectives lazy   a   beautiful
                the   young   happy

7. _____.

8. _____.

Adverbs   daily   loudly   often
                never   gently   happily

9. _____.

10. _____.

Prepositions on   with   from
                 before   to   after

11. _____.

12. _____.

Conjunctions	and	but	or
	for	nor	yet

13. _____ .

14. _____ .

Interjections	help	hooray	stop
	wow	oh	ouch

15. _____ .

16. _____ .

☞ *Review the sentences you wrote with a classmate. Record your score.*

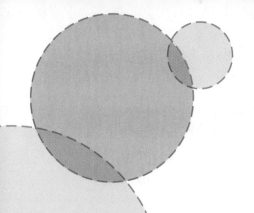

UNIT 3
CAPITALIZATION

WHAT YOU WILL LEARN

When you finish this unit, you will be able to:
- Write uppercase and lowercase letters.
- Understand the capitalization rules.
- Write sentences using the capitalization rules.

USING CAPITAL LETTERS

Capitalization is using capital letters. Capital letters are also called *uppercase letters*. Letters not capitalized are called *lowercase letters*. Handwritten letters in uppercase and lowercase would be written as shown in Illustration 3-1.

Illustration 3-1	
Handwritten Uppercase and Lowercase Letters	*Aa Bb Cc Dd Ee* *Ff Gg Hh Ii Jj* *Kk Ll Mm Nn* *Oo Pp Qq Rr Ss* *Tt Uu Vv Ww Xx* *Yy Zz*

31

✔ CHECKPOINT 3-1

YOUR GOAL:
Write 52 letters.

Practice writing the alphabet. Use a pencil or pen. Write uppercase and lowercase letters as shown in Illustration 3-1.

☞ *Check your work. Record your score.*

On a computer, uppercase and lowercase letters would be keyed as shown in Illustration 3-2.

Illustration 3-2

Uppercase and Lowercase Letters

Uppercase
A B C D E F G H I J K L M N O P Q R S T U V W X Y Z

Lowercase
a b c d e f g h i j k l m n o p q r s t u v w x y z

EVOLUTION OF WRITING—The Magic Alphabet

An alphabet is a collection of symbols. They are known as *letters* in writing. In speaking, they are known as *sounds*. The term *alphabet* was first used by the early Christian scholars Tertullian and St. Jerome. The word is from the first two letters of the Greek alphabet—*alpha* and *beta*. An alphabet is the foundation of all verbal and written communication.

BASIC CAPITALIZATION RULES

Capitalization helps make your writing and ideas clear. Capital letters are used for two main purposes. They show the beginning of a sentence and they show that a noun is a proper noun. You will recall that a proper noun is the name of a specific person, place, or thing. The following are basic capitalization rules:

1. **Always capitalize the first word in a sentence.**

   He gave an inspiring speech.
   Janice is taking piano lessons.

2. **Always capitalize the first word of a direct quotation.**

   The interviewer said, "We would like to hire you."
   Mr. Herrera asked, "Can you begin working on Monday?"

3. **Always capitalize the name of a specific person, place, or thing.**

Person:	Jesse Jackson
	George Washington
Place:	New Orleans
	St. Louis, Missouri
Thing:	Empire State Building
	Eiffel Tower

4. **Always capitalize the days of the week and months of the year.**

   Monday   Wednesday   February   June   December

5. **Always capitalize special days—holidays and religious holidays.**

Veteran's Day	Hanukkah
Father's Day	Thanksgiving Day

Illustration 3-3 shows capitalization rules 1–5 used in a sentence.

Illustration 3-3

Capitalization
Rules 1–5

RULES 1, 2, 3, 4, and 5*

1
The librarian told the students,
2   3   3
"Please remember the Main Library
4   4
is open Monday through Saturday
5   5   5
and only closed on New Year's Day."

The librarian. . .
Please. . . Main
Library. . .
Monday through. . .
New Year's Day

*The number above some words is the number of the capitalization rule.

✔ CHECKPOINT 3-2

YOUR GOAL:
Get 20 or more
answers correct.

Put a check mark in the space provided next to each sentence that is capitalized correctly. On the lines following the sentences, write the words that should be capitalized. The first one is completed as an example.

● _____ a. Neal was born on friday, october 2, 1961.

   ✓ _____ b. He was born in Lexington, Kentucky.

   _____ c. he was delivered by dr. cynthia kline.

_____ **Friday, October** _____

_____ **Dr. Cynthia Kline** _____

1. _____ a. Classes will not be held on new year's Day.

   _____ b. We were honored by a visit from the Queen of England.

   _____ c. The lincoln memorial is located in washington, d. c.

_____

_____

2. _____ a. Palm Sunday is the Sunday before Easter.

   _____ b. The golden gate bridge is in san francisco.

   _____ c. julianne takes swimming lessons every saturday.

   _____

   _____

3. _____ a. Conchita will be attending the class on monday.

   _____ b. Louis Armstrong played the trumpet.

   _____ c. He is a bus driver in detroit, michigan.

   _____

   _____

4. _____ a. Eduardo lopez agreed to work on christmas day.

   _____ b. we will be closed during passover.

   _____ c. Independence Day is on July 4.

   _____

   _____

5. _____ a. Mrs. Wong asked, "what computer software do you use?"

   _____ b. mark twain said, "When in doubt, tell the truth."

   _____ c. "Don't laugh at age, pray to reach it too," is an old Chinese proverb.

   _____

   _____

☞ *Check your work. Record your score.*

If your score is 20 or more, continue with the rules. If your score is less than 20, go back and review rules 1–5. Redo the sentences before continuing.

6. **Always capitalize all important words in titles.**

> Prince of Wales   Governor of New York
> Prime Minister Bhutto   President Corazon Aquino

 7. **Always capitalize names of businesses, organizations, institutions, and government agencies.**

> Bank of America   American Red Cross
> Burger King   United Nations
> Grand Auto   Institute of Technology

 8. **Always capitalize copyrighted names, brand names, and trade-marks.**

> Jell-O   Kleenex tissues
> Toyota Celica   Michelin tires

9. **Always capitalize religions, ethnic groups, and languages.**

> Disciples of Christ   Spanish
> Hmong   African American
> Asian   English

10. **Always capitalize relatives such as mother, father, aunt, and uncle when these words are used as names, or with specific names.**

> My Uncle Gerald is a good cook.
> Is Grandmother going with us?
> Dad, Mom is working late today.

Illustration 3-4 shows capitalization rules 6–10 used in sentences.

Illustration 3-4

Capitalization Rules 6–10

RULES 6, 7, 8, 9, and 10*

The Prime Minister of Japan visited
the United Nations. He was escorted
in a Mercedes limousine. His
Aunt Murasaki, who travels with him,
speaks English as well as Japanese.

*The number above some words is the number of the capitalization rule.

CHECKPOINT 3-3

YOUR GOAL:
Get 20 or more
answers correct.

Put a check mark in the space provided next to each sentence that is capitalized correctly. On the lines following the sentences, write the words that should be capitalized. The first one is completed as an example.

● _____ a. Roberto speaks chinese and japanese fluently.

_____ b. John and kim work as stockbrokers for stock corporation.

__✓__ b. Aunt Jane lives in Arizona.

_____ **Chinese, Japanese** _____

_____ **Kim, Stock Corporation** _____

1. _____ a. Katherine is employed by the U. S. department of defense.

_____ b. Harvey's hamburgers were served to the baseball players.

_____ c. The red cross provided food and shelter to the flood victims.

_____

_____

2. _____ a. Ron is washing his volkswagen rabbit.

_____ b. The dentist recommended Bright or No-Cavity toothpaste.

_____ c. Tammy bought the computer at compu-shop.

_____

_____

3. _____ a. The duchess of york will visit the united states.

_____ b. President lyndon b. johnson was from texas.

_____ c. Miss Ochoa was named Teacher of the Year.

_____

_____

4. _____ a. The students were puerto rican, Laotian, cuban, and korean.

  _____ b. Michael attends the first baptist church.

  _____ c. Grace likes Mexican and Italian food.

  _____

  _____

5. _____ a. My friend francisco lives in South America.

  _____ b. Our Aunt Alice gave a St. Patrick's Day party.

  _____ c. Mom, dad is taking us bowling.

  _____

  _____

☞ *Check your work. Record your score.*

    If your score is 20 or more, continue with the rules. If your score is less than 20, go back and review rules 6–10. Redo the sentences before continuing.

➡ 11. **Always capitalize the first letter of each word in the salutation of a letter.**
   Dear Dr. Wolfe Dear Mrs. Campos Dear Kuniko

➡ 12. **Always capitalize the first word in the complimentary closing of a letter.**
   Sincerely   Very truly yours   Sincerely yours

➡ 13. **Always capitalize initials and abbreviations of names and places.**
   John Fitzgerald Kennedy—J. F. Kennedy
   United States of America—USA
   International Business Machines—IBM

EVOLUTION OF WRITING—The Magic Alphabet

The Greek alphabet influenced many other alphabets. One of those was the Latin alphabet. The Latin alphabet was adapted to many languages. Among those languages are English, German, Swedish, Danish, Norwegian, Dutch, Italian, French, Spanish, Portuguese, Romanian, Polish, Czech, and Hungarian.

14. **Capitalize north, south, east, and west *only* when they refer to specific regions.**
   the East Coast   the Midwest
   She was a popular candidate in the South.

 15. **Always capitalize the pronoun I.**
   What time should I call?
   My brother and I are twins.

Illustration 3-5 shows capitalization rules 11–15 used in a sentence.

Illustration 3-5

Capitalization
Rules 11–15

RULES 11, 12, 13, 14, and 15*

   11   11
Dear Melanie,
15
I am planning a business trip to
         14   15   13
the East Coast. When I am in N.Y.

from June 12–14, let's have dinner.
15   15
I will call when I arrive.
              12
Sincerely yours,
Cameron

*The number above some words is the number of the capitalization rule.

CHECKPOINT 3-4

YOUR GOAL:
Get 10 or more
answers correct.

Put a check mark in the space provided next to each sentence that is capitalized correctly. On the lines following the sentences, write the words that should be capitalized. The first one is completed as an example.

● _____ a. The abbreviation for the united states of america is usa.

 _____ b. Mayume will be transferred to the west coast.

 ___✓___ c. I have a savings account at American Savings.

United, States, America, USA

West Coast

1. _____ a. Dear ms. kartes

 _____ b. Dear reverend okamoto

 _____ c. Dear Assemblyman Brown

_____

_____

2. _____ a. sincerely yours

 _____ b. Yours very truly

 _____ c. respectfully

_____

_____

3. _____ a. epcot (Environmental Prototype Community of Tomorrow)

 _____ b. fdr (Franklin D. Roosevelt)

 _____ c. NASA (National Aeronautics and Space Administration)

_____

_____

4. _____ a. Ally grew up in a small mining town in the west.

   _____ b. The thundershowers settled into the Northwest.

   _____ c. Kyle will be going to college in the south.

   _____

   _____

5. _____ a. I is a pronoun.

   _____ b. Margarita said happily, "i will be 13 this year."

   _____ c. My sister and i will be taking a math class.

   _____

   _____

☞ *Check your work. Record your score.*

If your score is 10 or more, go on to ACTIVITY 3-1. If your score is less than 10, go back and review rules 11–15. Redo the sentences before continuing.

WHAT YOU HAVE LEARNED

As a result of completing this unit, you have learned:
- How to write uppercase and lowercase letters.
- The basic capitalization rules.
- How to write sentences using the capitalization rules.

ACTIVITY 3-1   **YOUR GOAL:** Get 70 or more answers correct.

Underline the first letter of the words that should be capitalized in each of the following sentences. The first one is completed as an example.

- Videocassette recorders are manufactured by sony, kenwood, and panasonic.

1. J. c. penny is having an after-christmas sale.

2. We will be going to disneyland on memorial day.

3. The american heart association is having a walk-a-thon on saturday.

4. The translator speaks german, french, and spanish.

5. uncle bob, a tennis player, manages the scottsdale racquet club.

6. The rams, vikings, and broncos are names of football teams.

7. Leroy martinez is a cashier at save money market.

8. Income tax forms are mailed to the internal revenue service.

9. The first african-american governor was elected in 1989 in richmond, virginia.

10. "while you were in school," Mrs. Lueng asked, "did you take keyboarding and accounting?"

11. The salutation in the letter was, dear ms. tyson.

12. Tod is a computer engineer for high-tech, inc. in colorado.

13. sherry drives an essex convertible.

14. The united nations is located in new york.

15. Prince charles is next in line to become the king of england.

16. Martha asked, "would you like a coca-cola or a pepsi?"

17. Pauline and tim's wedding was held at the first methodist church.

18. Pete and elizabeth will be applying for a home loan at milwaukee savings and loan.

19. The pilot is being transferred from the east coast to the west coast.

20. The supervisor closed the letter by saying, "sincerely yours."

21. thanksgiving day is always on a thursday.

22. i emigrated from cambodia last january.

23. The abbreviation for the Immigration and Naturalization Service is ins.

24. The radial tires on the corvino are made by supertire.

25. The largest state in the united states is alaska.

☞ *Check your work. Record your score.*

ACTIVITY 3-2   YOUR GOAL: Write 10 sentences.

Write a sentence about each of your favorite things in the spaces provided. Use words with capital letters in each sentence. The first one is completed as an example.

● **car** _____ I like to drive my Range Rover. _____

1. **food** _____

2. **movie** _____

3. **beverage** _____

4. **sport** _____

5. **hobby** _____

6. **book** _____

7. **vacation** _____

8. **holiday** _____

9. **pet** _____

10. **friend** _____

☞ *Review your sentences with a classmate. Record your score.*

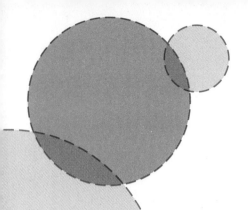

UNIT 4
PUNCTUATION

WHAT YOU WILL LEARN

When you finish this unit, you will be able to:
- Identify punctuation marks.
- Punctuate sentences using the punctuation rules.

PUNCTUATION MARKS

To be an effective writer, you must clearly convey to the reader what you mean. **Punctuation marks** are symbols used to add clarity to writing. Understanding basic punctuation rules will help you in reading as well as in writing.

There are 12 commonly used punctuation marks. To help you identify them, study Illustration 4-1.

Illustration 4-1				
Commonly Used Punctuation Marks	Apostrophe	'	Hyphen	-
	Colon	:	Parentheses	( )
	Comma	,	Period	.
	Dash	—	Question Mark	?
	Ellipsis Marks	...	Quotation Marks	" "
	Exclamation Point	!	Semicolon	;

✔ CHECKPOINT 4-1

YOUR GOAL:
Get 25 or more answers correct.

The following sentences from advertisements show how punctuation marks are used. Underline the punctuation marks in each. Write the name for each punctuation mark in the space provided. The first one is completed as an example.

Here's an eye-opening offer. • apostrophe

 hyphen

 period

**Is this the year
you'll buy a home?**   1. _____

 _____

It's Ripe and Ready!   2. _____

 _____

Portable Color TV—Never Priced Lower! 3. _____

 _____

Lighter, airier, and
 crunchier.   4. _____

 _____

 _____

Want to retire someday?   5. _____

**Buy now . . . these prices
 won't get any lower!**   6. _____

 _____

 _____

**We'll help you
make it to the top.**   7. _____

 _____

Chicken Teriyaki from scratch: 8. _____
1 hour, 39 minutes.   _____

                                       _____

"That'll be $131.20, please."   9. _____

                                       _____

                                       _____

                                       _____

                                       _____

Semi-annual sale!   10. _____

                                       _____

Help keep your teeth for life!   11. _____

☞ *Check your work. Record your score.*

RULES FOR USING PUNCTUATION MARKS

Knowing the rules for using punctuation marks will help you write more clearly. Using the correct punctuation marks makes it easier for the reader to understand what you have written. The following are rules for the 12 most commonly used punctuation marks.

Apostrophe

An apostrophe (') is used in writing contractions. A **contraction** is a shorter way of writing some pairs of words.

Examples: *are not* is written *aren't*

I am is written *I'm*

An apostrophe is used to show possession.

Examples: Donna's motorcycle.

The child's toy.

Colon ━━━━━━━━━━━━━━━━━━━━━━━━━━

A colon (:) may be used after the salutation of a business letter.

Examples: Dear Ms. Gilmore:

Dear Dr. Alvarez:

A colon is used between hours and minutes in expressing time.

Examples: 8:30 A.M.   5:45 P.M.

A colon is used to introduce a list.

Example: Nancy's salad included her three favorite vegetables: avocados, mushrooms, and tomatoes.

✓ CHECKPOINT 4-2

YOUR GOAL:
Get 4 or more answers correct.

Insert an apostrophe (') or a colon (:) in each of the following sentences. The first one is completed as an example:

● I'm not eating any more broccoli.

1. She cant attend the meeting.

2. Dear Ms. Gipson This is an application for employment.

3. Whats so funny about that?

4. He enjoys playing these games volleyball, tennis, and basketball.

5. The time is exactly 103 P.M.

☞ *Check your work. Record your score.*

Comma

A comma (,) is used between the city and state. In a sentence, a comma is also used after the state.

Examples: Baltimore, Maryland
They worked in Baltimore, Maryland, for five years.

A comma is used between the day of the month and the year. In a sentence, a comma is also used after the year.

Examples: July 4, 1776
July 4, 1776, was when the Declaration of Independence was adopted.

A comma is used between the words or groups of words in a series, including before the words *and* or *or*.

Example: Salad, soup, or dessert comes with the meal.

A comma is used to separate a direct quotation from the rest of the sentence.

Example: Connie said, "Thank you for helping."

A comma may be used in a business letter after the close. In a personal letter, a comma may be used after the opening and the close.

Examples: Sincerely yours,
Dear Lisa,

A comma is used in numbers.

Examples: 3,983
569,294

A comma is used to set off an appositive. An **appositive** is a word or group of words that rename a noun.

Example: Mr. Howard, her math teacher, has a sense of humor.

A comma is used after an introductory word or phrase to separate it from the rest of the sentence.

Examples: Yes, they are going to see a movie.
After the movie, they are going to study.

A comma is used before a conjunction in a compound sentence.

Example: Mitch and Dennis both work, and they get good grades.

Dash

The dash (—) is used to indicate a sudden break or change in thought. The dash may be used in place of the comma to indicate a special emphasis. On the typewriter or computer, use two hyphens to make a dash. There is no space before or after a dash.

Example: Leah—an adult student—wants to become an engineer.

A dash may be used to emphasize a word, series of words, phrase, or clause.

Example: In addition to work and family—we are thankful for good health.

CHECKPOINT 4-3

YOUR GOAL:
Get 5 or more answers correct.

Insert a comma (,) or a dash (—) in each of the following sentences. The first one is completed as an example.

● Clarence was born on March 2, 1980.

1. He won two million dollars to be paid in one lump sum.

2. The U.S. Coast Guard protector of America's shores was held responsible.

3. Her home was in Portland Oregon.

4. Reading writing and math are important basic skills.

5. His father said "Please drive carefully."

☞ Check your work. Record your score.

Ellipsis Marks

An ellipsis (. . .) is used to show when one or more words are omitted in quoted material or an unfinished sentence. Use three ellipsis marks if they are used to interrupt the sentence. Use four ellipsis marks (one as a period) if they are used to finish the sentence.

Examples: The speaker said, "Love your work . . . and follow your dream."

The salary range varies, and will depend on work experience.
The salary range varies. . . .

Exclamation Point ━━━━━━━━━━━

The exclamation point (!) is used to express a strong feeling. It is used at the end of a word, a phrase, or a sentence.

Examples: Help!   Dad!   Help!

✔ CHECKPOINT 4-4

YOUR GOAL:
Get 5 or more answers correct.

Insert ellipsis marks (...) or an exclamation point (!) in each of the following sentences. The first one is completed as an example.

● Hurry! We are going to miss the bus.

1. The latest development seemed to catch few by surprise.

2. Wow Her singing was really awesome.

3. He said, "These are the needing a response."

4. Fire Fire

5. Wait I'll be there in a minute.

☞ *Check your work. Record your score.*

Hyphen ━━━━━━━━━━━

A hyphen (-) is used to join the words in compound numbers.

Examples: twenty-eight   thirty-two

A hyphen is used between numbers in a fraction.

Examples: one-fourth   five-eighths

A hyphen is used between two adjectives when they are written before the word they modify.

Examples: heavy-duty wrench   double-spaced copy

A hyphen is used after the prefixes *self* and *ex* when *ex* means former.

Examples: self-sufficient   ex-president

A hyphen is used with compound words. A hyphen is also used for dividing a word at the end of a line of writing. Because there is no simple rule for hyphenating compound words, consult a dictionary. Or, you may refer to *Punctuation, Capitalization, and Handwriting* by Renae Humburg, South-Western Publishing Co., 1992.

Parentheses

Parentheses [( )] are used around words included in a sentence to add information. These words help make the idea clearer.

Example: The Duong's children (Kim and Tran) speak Laotian.

Parentheses are used to enclose letters or figures that mark items in a series.

Example: They came up with three choices: (1) visit the Grand Canyon, (2) take a cruise to the Bahamas, or (3) fly to London.

✔ CHECKPOINT 4-5

YOUR GOAL:
Get 9 or more answers correct.

Insert a hyphen (-) or parentheses [( )] in each of the following sentences. The first one is completed as an example.

- She measured two-thirds of a yard.

1. The three metals included were: 1 steel, 2 chrome, and 3 aluminum.

2. Three fourths of the machines were automatic.

3. It was a well known organization.

4. Five of the students Megan, Noriko, Chris, Tony, and Liza were awarded first prizes.

5. Success has made him very self satisfied.

☞ *Check your work. Record your score.*

Period

The period (.) is the most frequently used punctuation mark. A period is used at the end of a sentence.

Example: The Castros have been married for 25 years.

A period is used after an initial and after an abbreviated word.

Examples: C. J. Barrett   Mrs.   Dr.   P.M.   Co.

Question Mark

A question mark (?) is used at the end of a sentence that asks a direct question. A question mark should not be used after an indirect question.

Examples: What are your plans after you finish the cosmetology training?
She was asked if she wanted a full-time job.

CHECKPOINT 4-6

YOUR GOAL:
Get 7 or more answers correct.

Insert a period (.) or question mark (?) in each of the following sentences. The first one is completed as an example.

• Sheila asked, "Are we going at 7 A.M. or 7 P.M.?"

1. He was introduced to Mr Reynolds

2. What is the name of that song

3. Where did they live from 1975–1985

4. Mitch, a word processor, works from 8:30 AM to 4:30 PM

5. How many applicants are there for the job

☞ *Check your work. Record your score.*

EVOLUTION OF WRITING—The First Written Language

The earliest known written language is that of ancient Sumer. The Sumerians were members of a Babylonian society established around 4000 B.C. Their culture was preserved using a system of writing on clay tablets. This writing, known as cuneiform, consists of shapes and designs that resemble drawings, as compared to modern letter forms. The many languages used today can be traced back to the language of the ancient Sumerians.

Quotation Marks

Quotation marks (" ") are used before and after a direct quotation. Quotation marks are used to emphasize certain words. Commas and periods are inside the quotation marks. A question mark is inside the quotation marks if the quoted material is a question.

Examples: "Yes," said Yuki, "Sadako is my sister."
He thinks his work is "better."

Quotation marks are used to punctuate titles of poems, songs, magazine articles, stories, and chapters of books or newspapers.

Examples: The song, "We Are the World," is a popular international song.
The section entitled, "Interviewing Tips," was very helpful.

Semicolon

A semicolon (;) is used to join two independent clauses not connected by a conjunction like *and, but, for,* or *or.*

Example: Albert gets up early; this is the best time for him to study.

A semicolon is used to join two independent clauses that are connected by a transitional expression. Some transitional expressions include: *however, therefore, meanwhile, finally,* and *for example.*

Example: The Kleins are going to Canada on vacation; however, their children will stay at home.

✔ CHECKPOINT 4-7

YOUR GOAL:
Get 5 or more answers correct.

Insert quotation marks (" ") or a semicolon (;) in each of the following sentences. The first one is completed as an example.

- They saw the play, "Phantom of the Opera."

1. The instructor said, Be positive, confident, and have a can-do attitude.

2. The trio is talented Bill on piano, Greg on bass, and Joyce on drums play well together.

3. He is an early riser however, he is always late for work.

4. The officer asked, How did the accident happen?

5. The train was late it arrived two hours behind schedule.

☞ *Check your work. Record your score.*

WHAT YOU HAVE LEARNED

As a result of completing this unit, you have learned to:
- Identify the 12 commonly used punctuation marks.
- Correctly use punctuation marks in sentences.

ACTIVITY 4-1   **YOUR GOAL:** Get 65 or more answers correct.

Read the following paragraphs. Underline the punctuation marks used in each line. Write the number of punctuation marks used in each line in the space provided. The first one is completed as an example.

BALANCING WORK AND FAMILY LIFE

- Mr. and Mrs. Mike Garcia both have full-time _____3_____
1. jobs. Mrs. Garcia also goes to school. _____
2. She is learning English; she is taking an _____
3. English-as-a-Second-Language (ESL) course. _____
4. The Garcias have three teenage children. _____
5. Their names are Hortencia, Mañuel, and _____
6. Carlos. Like many parents, they balance _____
7. working, going to school, and spending time _____
8. with their children. _____
9. Do you have the same situation? Do you _____
10. want to spend more time with your family? _____
11. Do your children share with family _____
12. chores? Some parents say, _____
13. "It's easier to do it myself." Other _____
14. parents say, "I can't do everything," or _____
15. "I need help!" _____
16. Mr. and Mrs. Garcia's children help with _____
17. family chores. Mrs. Garcia uses a calendar _____
18. to plan who does what job around the house. _____
19. Some of the chores that Hortencia, Mañuel, _____
20. and Carlos help with are (1) washing _____

21. clothes, (2) shopping for groceries,   _____

22. (3) cleaning house, (4) preparing meals,   _____

23. (5) washing dishes, and (6) mowing the lawn.   _____

24. Training the children to help with family   _____

25. chores has helped the Garcia children develop   _____

26. responsibility. They are running their   _____

27. household jointly; they also have more   _____

28. time together as a family. Mr. and Mrs. Garcia   _____

29. realize that two important things in their   _____

30. life—their jobs and their family—are   _____

31. very related. What are you doing to   _____

32. balance your work and family life?   _____

☞ *Check your work. Record your score.*

ACTIVITY 4-2   YOUR GOAL: Get 45 or more answers correct.

Insert the proper punctuation marks in each of the following sentences. The first one is completed as an example.

● Your personal network—friends, family, and co-workers—can give you emotional support.

1. Youre not alone

2. Many older workers want to continue working retirement is only one option

3. The three jobs hes qualified for are secretarial accounting and sales

4. The job required these basic skills 1 spelling 2 math and 3 writing skills

5. Maybe youll get lucky and find a job right away

6. Does she prefer full time or part time work

7. The response No, youre not what were looking for, may be hard on your ego

8. Your self confidence is reflected in your appearance

9. Finding the right job takes time patience and hard work

10. Congratulations You have been hired

11. The interviewer continued then asked the applicant to respond

12. Hooray I passed the test

13. He didnt get the job however the interview was a good experience

14. The exam will be given on June l4 at 830 AM

15. Many women and older workers are re entering the work force

☞ *Check your work. Record your score.*

PART TWO
DEVELOPING YOUR WRITING SKILLS

UNIT 5
WRITING SENTENCES

UNIT 6
PARAGRAPHS

UNIT 7
NOTES AND MESSAGES

UNIT 5
WRITING SENTENCES

WHAT YOU WILL LEARN

When you finish this unit, you will be able to:
- Write simple sentences.
- Write compound sentences.
- Write more successfully.

CREATING SENTENCES

Writing is a building process. You build sentences by putting together a series of words. Sentences can be short, medium, or long. A variety of sentence lengths will make your writing more interesting. In Unit 1, you learned about the sentence and its parts. In this unit, you will experience writing simple and compound sentences.

WRITING SIMPLE SENTENCES

A sentence is a group of words that expresses a complete thought. A complete sentence has a subject and a predicate. All the words related to the subject are part of the complete subject. All the words related to the predicate are part of the complete predicate. Within each basic part of the sentence is a key word or words called the *simple subject* and *simple predicate*. The simple predicate is also called the *verb*.

The simple subject always answers the question *who* or *what*. The verb tells something about the subject.

A **simple sentence** has one independent clause. An **independent clause** is a group of words that has a subject and a verb. The following sentences are simple sentences. A line is drawn between the subject and the predicate. The simple subject is underlined once and the verb twice.

1. My <u>name</u> | <u>is</u> Midori Tanaka.
2. <u>I</u> | <u>am</u> 35 years old.
3. <u>I</u> | <u>was born</u> in Kyoto, Japan.
4. <u>I</u> | <u>have been married</u> for 10 years.
5. <u>We</u> | <u>live</u> in Columbus, Ohio.
6. <u>We</u> | <u>have</u> a daughter and a son.
7. <u>We</u> | <u>live</u> in a three-bedroom apartment.
8. My <u>hobbies</u> | <u>include</u> gardening and painting.
9. <u>I</u> | <u>am looking</u> for a job as a dental assistant.
10. <u>I</u> | <u>have</u> five years of work experience.

✔ CHECKPOINT 5-1

YOUR GOAL:
Write 10 simple sentences.

Answer each question in the following list by writing a simple sentence in the space provided. Be sure to include a simple subject and a verb in each sentence. Underline the simple subject once and the verb twice. The first one is completed as an example.

● **What do you like to read?**

1. What is your name?

2. How old are you?

3. Where were you born?

4. If you are married, how long have you been married?

5. Where do you live?

6. Do you have any children?

7. Do you live in a house, apartment, or condominium?

8. What are your favorite hobbies?

9. If you are looking for a job, what kind of job are you looking for?

10. How many years of work experience do you have?

- <u>I like</u> to read the newspaper.

1. _____ .

2. _____ .

3. _____ .

4. _____ .

5. _____ .

6. _____ .

7. _____ .

8. _____ .

9. _____ .

10. _____ .

☞ *Review your sentences with a classmate. Record your score.*

WRITING COMPOUND SENTENCES

A **compound sentence** combines two or more ideas into the same sentence. Compound sentences are longer and more complex. A compound sentence has two or more independent clauses. As previously stated, an independent clause is a group of words that has a subject and a verb. A simple sentence used as part of a compound sentence is called an *independent clause*. Independent clauses in a compound sentence are joined by a conjunction, adverb, or semicolon.

If the clauses are joined by a conjunction (*and, but, or, for, nor, yet,* and *so*) a comma precedes the conjunction.

Examples of Simple Sentences:
We need doctors.
We need nurses even more.

Example of Compound Sentence:
We need doctors, but we need nurses even more.

If the clauses are joined by an **adverb** (*furthermore, therefore, thus, however, otherwise, in addition*), a semicolon is used before the adverb, and a comma after.

Examples of Simple Sentences:

George was hungry.
He ordered a turkey sandwich, potato salad, and apple pie.

Example of Compound Sentence:

George was hungry; therefore, he ordered a turkey sandwich, potato salad, and apple pie.

✔ CHECKPOINT 5-2

YOUR GOAL:
Get 4 or more answers correct.

Combine each pair of simple sentences to form a compound sentence in the space provided. Use the word in the parentheses to write your sentence. The first one is completed as an example.

● Staycee will graduate in May. She will be looking for a job in Boston. (and)

_____Staycee will graduate in May, and she will be_____

_____looking for a job in Boston._____

1. Her parents will help her buy a new car. She will pay for the car insurance. (however)

   _____

   _____

2. She has rented an apartment. She wants a roommate to share expenses. (therefore)

   _____

   _____

3. Jason completed the job application. He took a math and grammar test. (and)

   _____

   _____

4. He could operate the computer. He would not meet one requirement of the job. (otherwise)

    _____

    _____

5. The work hours are flexible. He will have to work one weekend a month. (however)

    _____

    _____

☞ *Check your work. Record your score.*

SUGGESTIONS FOR SUCCESSFUL WRITING

What you write and the way you write tell the reader about **YOU.** Choosing the right words is necessary for setting the tone of your message. What you say or write should be accurate, clear, and appropriate for the reader.

Correct Grammar

Using correct grammar in writing is important for two reasons. First, incorrect grammar can make a poor impression on the reader. Second, a written message can sometimes be read in more than one way because of incorrect grammar. It is also important that all your words be spelled correctly.

Correct Capitalization and Punctuation

Correct capitalization and punctuation should be used. Rules for capitalization and punctuation presented in Units 3 and 4 should be followed.

WRITING GEMS—Quotes Worth Repeating

"You must do the thing you think you cannot do."

Eleanor Roosevelt, American Statesperson

"Whatever you are; be a good one."

Abraham Lincoln, 16th U.S. President

Subject-Verb Agreement

In writing sentences, the verb must agree in number with its subject. A subject and a verb agree in number when they are both singular or both plural. **Number** means *singular* (one) or *plural* (more than one). A list of singular and plural verbs is shown in Illustration 5-1.

Illustration 5-1

Singular and Plural Verbs

SINGULAR	PLURAL	SINGULAR	PLURAL
is	are	was	were
does	do	has	have
wishes	wish	calls	call
runs	run	helps	help
goes	go	says	say
cooks	cook	seems	seem
flies	fly	makes	make
finds	find	writes	write
talks	talk	walks	walk
carries	carry	draws	draw

Example:

The *report* (subject) by the committee chair *has* (verb) been printed.

(The subject *report* is singular; therefore, the singular verb *has* is used.)

Example:

The *reports* (subject), as well as the booklet, *have* (verb) to be finished by Friday.

(The subject *reports* is plural; therefore, the plural verb *have* is used.)

Noun and Pronoun Agreement

In Unit 2, you learned that a pronoun takes the place of a noun or refers to a noun. The pronoun must agree with its antecedent. **Antecedent** is the noun to which the pronoun refers. The noun and pronoun must agree in number and in gender. **Gender** refers to feminine (she), masculine (he), or neuter (it). When the antecedent's gender is unknown, use his or her.

Examples:

Dr. Lenora Flores couldn't remember where *she* had laid *her* stethoscope. (*she* and *her* are singular—they refer to *Dr. Lenora Flores*)

(The *doctors* said *they* had lowered *their* fees. [*they* and *their* are plural—they refer to *doctors*])

CHECKPOINT 5-3

YOUR GOAL:
Get 8 or more answers correct.

Choose the correct pronoun or verb in parentheses in the following sentences. Write each pronoun or verb in the space provided. The first one is completed as an example.

_____she_____ • Was it you or (**she/her**) who had a perfect score?

_____ 1. "Who broke the machine?" "Not (**I/me**)."

_____ 2. Before a person signs a contract, (**he/they**) ought to read it.

_____ 3. Perry and (**I/me**) closed all the windows.

_____ 4. The two finalists, Kate and (**he/him**), received $300.

_____ 5. A quart (**seem/seems**) more than enough for four servings.

_____ 6. The story (**has/have**) been told many times.

_____ 7. Uncle Walter's favorite dessert (**is/are**) ice cream.

_____ 8. The students in the marketing course (**go/goes**) on monthly field trips.

_____ 9. His interest in electronics (**surprise/surprises**) me.

_____ 10. The spelling of all the names on the list (**has/have**) to be checked.

☞ *Check your work. Record your score.*

Sentence Structure

The sentence is the basic unit of communication. Using correct sentence structure will help you speak and write sentences that communicate your ideas more clearly. Sentence structures to avoid using are sentence fragments and run-on sentences.

◀ **WRITING GEMS—Quote Worth Repeating**

"Writing is for reading. Better writing makes better reading, and better reading makes better writing."

Edgar Dale, Communication Expert

Sentence Fragment

A **sentence fragment** is a group of words that does not sound complete. It usually does not tell *who* or *what* someone or something did, or *what* happened. When a fragment is read, it seems as if something is missing.

Example: Jogging down the road. (The thought is incomplete. Who is jogging down the road?)

To make this fragment a sentence, the writer must complete the thought. The following sentence is now complete because it expresses a complete thought.

Correct: Lynette was jogging down the road.

Run-On Sentence

A **run-on sentence** is two or more sentences that run together because of incorrect or no punctuation.

Example: Lee forgot to set his alarm, he was late for work.

Correct:
Lee forgot to set his alarm; therefore, he was late for work.
Lee was late for work because he forgot to set his alarm.
Lee forgot to set his alarm; he was late for work.

✔ **CHECKPOINT 5-4**

YOUR GOAL:
Get 3 or more
answers correct.

In each pair of lines that follow, one is a fragment or run-on sentence; the other is a complete sentence. Put a check mark in the space provided next to each complete sentence. The first one is completed as an example.

● _____ a. Plays basketball after work.

_____✓____ b. Dimitri plays basketball after work.

1. _____ a. Dieted for a month.

   _____ b. She dieted for a month and didn't lose a pound.

2. _____ a. Wear safety goggles and gloves.

   _____ b. Welders need to wear safety goggles and gloves.

3. _____ a. That can't be Monika's paper she doesn't write that legibly.

   _____ b. That can't be Monika's paper because she doesn't write that legibly.

4. _____ a. George, my cousin, is secretary to the district attorney.

   _____ b. Secretary to the district attorney.

5. _____ a. Two of the students had to leave early they have after-school jobs.

   _____ b. Because they have after-school jobs, two of the students had to leave early.

☞ *Check your work. Record your score.*

WHAT YOU HAVE LEARNED

As a result of completing this unit, you have learned:
- To write simple and compound sentences.
- That successful writing includes using correct
  - capitalization and punctuation,
  - subject-verb agreement,
  - noun and pronoun agreement, and
  - sentence structure.
- The difference between a sentence fragment, a run-on sentence, and a complete sentence.

ACTIVITY 5-1 YOUR GOAL: Write 6 sentences.

Look at Illustrations 5-2 through 5-5. Each picture shows people working in different types of jobs. Write a simple sentence and a compound sentence describing each picture. Your sentences may include something you know about the job. You may also write about someone you know who has a job in that field. Write each of your sentences in the spaces provided. Sentences for the first illustration are completed as an example.

Illustration 5-2

School
Principal

- **Simple Sentence:**

  The school principal is talking to two students.

●● **Compound Sentence:**

  The principal is sitting, and the students are standing.

Illustration 5-3
Carpenter

1. **Simple Sentence:**

_____

2. **Compound Sentence:**

_____

Illustration 5-4

Salesperson

3. **Simple Sentence:**

    _____

4. **Compound Sentence:**

    _____

Illustration 5-5

Plumber

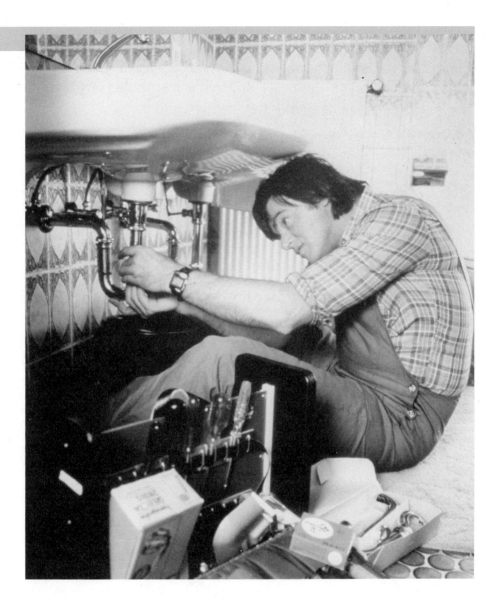

5. **Simple Sentence:**

_____

6. **Compound Sentence:**

_____

☞ _Review your sentences with a classmate. Record your score._

ACTIVITY 5-2　YOUR GOAL: Get 25 or more answers correct.

Underline the subject once and the verb twice in each of the following sentences. Indicate if the subject and verb are singular or plural in the space provided. The first one is completed as an example.

__Singular__　　● Sam <u>shares</u> the household chores.

_____　1.　They are ready for a busy sales year.

_____　2.　Mrs. Stein was promoted after three months.

_____　3.　The waiter carries heavy trays.

_____　4.　On Saturday, the custodians wash windows.

_____　5.　Yuan writes for the local newspaper.

_____　6.　We were asked to be on time.

_____　7.　She walks to work twice a week.

_____　8.　Gina and Armando drive trucks.

_____　9.　The office building has 15 stories.

_____　10.　His supervisor explains things very clearly.

☞ *Check your work. Record your score.*

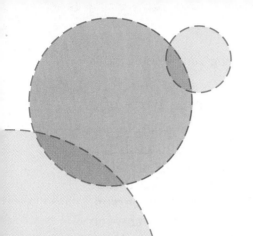

UNIT 6
PARAGRAPHS

WHAT YOU WILL LEARN

When you finish this unit, you will be able to:
- Identify the three parts of a paragraph.
- Write a short paragraph with one idea or subject.
- Follow the steps for writing paragraphs.

PARTS OF A PARAGRAPH

A **paragraph** is a group of sentences about one idea or subject. At least two sentences are needed to make a paragraph. A paragraph that has more than ten sentences is too long. Another paragraph should be started.

In Unit 5, you learned about writing sentences. In this unit, your writing skills will be expanded. You will be able to put sentences together to develop short paragraphs. Writing paragraphs, like everything you write, has to be planned. You need to think about what you want to say and how you want to say it.

There are three basic parts of a paragraph.

1. Beginning — The **topic sentence** is the first sentence in a paragraph. It tells the reader what the paragraph is going to be about. The topic sentence includes the subject of the paragraph.

2. Middle — The **body** is made up of sentences that support the topic of the paragraph. These sentences provide details that make the subject interesting to the reader.

3. End — The **ending** or **concluding sentence** comes after all details have been included in the body of the paragraph. This sentence reminds the reader of the topic of the paragraph.

The following paragraph illustrates the three parts of a paragraph.

Beginning (Topic Sentence)	<u>Apprenticeship is an on-the-job training system that prepares a person for a skilled occupation.</u> An apprentice works under the supervision of an experienced person. Training is a combination of on-the-job training and classroom instruction. Most
Middle (Body)	training takes two to five years. During this time, an apprentice learns new skills, gains experience, and assumes more job responsibilities. At the end of the training period, the apprentice is promoted to jour-neyperson. Apprenticeships are available in different trades, such as auto mechan-ics and welding. Apprenticeship programs are an important option for those who
End (Ending Sentence)	want a skilled occupation. <u>People who do not choose to work toward a college degree may consider an apprenticeship program.</u>

Putting together three parts of a paragraph takes a formula. The formula for writing paragraphs is shown in Illustration 6-1.

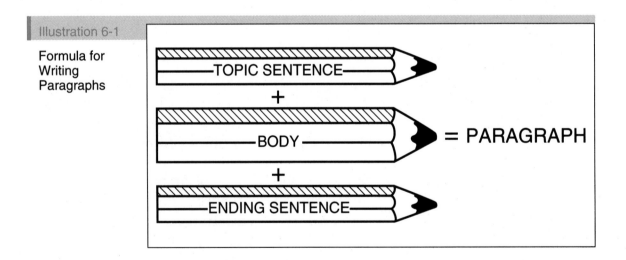

Illustration 6-1

Formula for Writing Paragraphs

◀ WRITING GEMS—Quote Worth Repeating

"Learning is a treasure that follows its owner everywhere."

Chinese Proverb

CHECKPOINT 6-1

YOUR GOAL:
Get 6 or more answers correct.

Read the following paragraphs. Underline the topic sentence once and the ending sentence twice in each of the following paragraphs.

1. Employability skills are necessary for every job in every business and industry. They are important in entry-level jobs or for job promotions. Employers have identified three areas of skills that are needed. They are (1) basic skills, which include English language and math skills; (2) pre-employment skills, which include career planning abilities and job hunting skills; and (3) work traits, which include interpersonal and personal management skills. Making the effort to learn these skills pays off. Remember, employability skills are needed in *every* job.

2. Recycling is one way we can help save our environment. Americans throw out 10 times their own weight in garbage every year. We throw out enough wood and paper to heat five million homes for 200 years. One ton of recycled paper saves 17 trees and 7,000 gallons of water. Each of us can help by recycling newspapers and copier, computer, and typing paper at home and at work. Recycling reduces air and water pollution and is one way to save our environment.

3. A detailed auto maintenance schedule can save you a lot of money. Auto manufacturers can suggest maintenance schedules that are based on either mileage or time. Your car can be serviced at the end of a certain time period or after a certain number of miles. Your maintenance schedule should include changing the oil and filter and checking the cooling system and the tire pressure. Brake pads also need to be inspected. Regular car care and detailed maintenance will result in fewer major repairs.

4. How smart are you when it comes to budgeting your income and handling money matters? Here are some basic steps you can take that will help you become an expert money manager: Know how much money you have, know what your expenses are, plan for both routine expenses and savings, write down what you spend, and follow your plan. By creating a budget, you will be managing your income effectively and wisely.

☞ *Check your work. Record your score.*

PARAGRAPHS—ONE IDEA OR SUBJECT

Paragraphs should be about one idea or subject. You need to be careful not to say too much. All the statements you make should refer to the subject you are writing about. A sentence should contain no unnecessary words. A paragraph should contain no unnecessary sentences. Remember to stick to the topic. Read the example paragraph in Illustration 6-2.

Illustration 6-2

Americans
Living
Longer

AMERICANS LIVING LONGER

In general, Americans are living longer. The number of people who are over age 65 is growing faster than other age groups. In 1981, people over age 65 made up 11.4 percent of the population. In the year 2000, this group is expected to grow to 13.1 percent. And in 2050, it will be as high as 21.7 percent. Although only 1 percent of the population lived to age 85 in 1981, by 2050 this number will be over 5.2 percent. The balance of different age groups is going to change greatly because Americans are living longer.

Source: U.S. Bureau of the Census

CHECKPOINT 6-2

YOUR GOAL:
Get 2 or more answers correct.

Put a check mark in the space provided next to the sentence that does not belong in each of the following paragraphs. The first one is completed as an example.

● _____ a. Jobs for people with no skills and no education are disappearing.

_____ b. Future employment will require some level of training and good communication skills.

_____ c. In addition, basic ability in math and reading will be needed.

___✓___ d. Fewer young people will enter the work force.

_____ e. Many jobs will require workers to give and receive directions and solve problems.

1. _____ a. When you communicate, you use actions as well as words.

   _____ b. For example, you use facial expressions, posture, and hand movements.

   _____ c. Just as you choose the clothing you wear, you must also choose the language that you use.

   _____ d. These non-verbal actions are referred to as *body language*.

   _____ e. The words and actions you use are your communication symbols.

2. _____ a. Stress is with us all the time.

   _____ b. Too much stress, however, can seriously affect your physical and mental well-being.

   _____ c. Stress can cause physical illness such as high blood pressure, ulcers, or even heart disease.

   _____ d. Physical stress from work or exercise is not likely to cause such ailments.

   _____ e. Sitting in gridlock traffic can be stressful.

   _____ f. Recognizing the early signs of stress and doing something about it can make a difference in the quality of your life.

3. _____ a. When preparing for the job interview, you should be aware of your personal appearance.

   _____ b. Your clothes, hairstyle, and overall appearance create an important first impression.

   _____ c. If you are uncertain as to how to dress for the interview, there are many books and magazines on the topic.

   _____ d. There are also books available that can help you with a job application.

   _____ e. Make your first impression work for you.

☞ *Check your work. Record your score.*

STEPS FOR WRITING PARAGRAPHS

A paragraph focuses on a single main idea. The sentences you write should be related. They should work together to explain or develop one main idea. Writing requires thought and planning. Follow these steps as a plan for writing paragraphs.

1. Decide what topic you are going to write about. Take time to think about what you want to say.

2. Put your main thoughts and ideas into words. Write them down. If it helps, read them aloud to yourself or to a classmate.

3. List the order of your ideas on paper.

4. Write the topic sentence. Then expand on that topic. This is the body of the paragraph. Write an ending sentence. Remember, the ending sentence should be about the main idea.

5. Revise your writing. Writing takes practice, so you may have to revise your writing several times. If a computer is available to you, keying your work will make revisions less time consuming.

6. Check your sentence structure—remember, no fragments or run-on sentences.

7. Proofread your writing for correct grammar, capitalization, punctuation, and spelling.

8. Make sure you have a topic sentence, body, and ending sentence.

9. Proofread your writing one last time.

WRITING GEMS—Famous Words from the Past
from *The Gettysburg Address*

"Four score and seven years ago our fathers brought forth on this continent a new nation, conceived in liberty, and dedicated to the proposition that all men are created equal. Now we are engaged in a great civil war, testing whether that nation, or any nation so conceived and so dedicated, can long endure. We are met on a great battlefield of that war. We have come to dedicate a portion of that field, as a final resting place for those who gave their lives that the nation might live. It is altogether fitting and proper that we should do this; but, in a larger sense, we cannot dedicate, we cannot consecrate, we cannot hallow, this ground. The brave men, living and dead, who struggled here, have consecrated it. . . ."

Abraham Lincoln, 16th U.S. President

CHECKPOINT 6-3

YOUR GOAL:
Get 6 or more answers correct.

The following is the list of steps for writing a paragraph. The steps are not in the correct order. Put the list in correct order by numbering the steps from 1 to 9 in the spaces provided. The first one is completed as an example.

● ____7____ Proofread for grammar, capitalization, punctuation, and spelling.

1. _____ Revise your writing.

2. _____ Write the topic sentence.

3. _____ Put your main thoughts and ideas into words.

4. _____ Proofread your writing one last time.

5. _____ Check your sentence structure.

6. _____ Decide what topic you are going to write about.

7. _____ List the order of your ideas on paper.

8. _____ Make sure you have a topic sentence, body, and ending sentence.

☞ *Check your work. Record your score.*

WHAT YOU HAVE LEARNED

As a result of completing this unit, you have learned:
● That paragraphs are made up of three parts—topic sentence, body, and ending sentence.
● That paragraphs should be about one idea or subject.
● The nine steps for writing paragraphs.

ACTIVITY 6-1 **YOUR GOAL:** Get 2 or more correct paragraphs.

Select three topics to write about from the following list. Put a check mark in the space provided next to each of the topics you choose.

_____ 1. Write the directions to your house.

_____ 2. Describe a memorable childhood experience.

_____ 3. Write about someone important in your life.

_____ 4. Write about a job you have had in the last 10 years.

_____ 5. Tell about your favorite sport or hobby.

_____ 6. Describe something you do well.

_____ 7. Write about a happy experience.

_____ 8. Write about your future goals.

_____ 9. Describe your favorite vacation.

_____ 10. Write about your culture and customs.

Write your paragraphs on a blank sheet of paper. Write one paragraph about each topic you selected. Follow the nine steps for writing paragraphs. A paragraph is written as an example.

- I enjoy helping my children with their schoolwork. I always encourage them. They receive praise for the things they do well. I try to make them feel good about themselves so that they will do their best. Sometimes, I meet with their teachers to go over their progress. I make sure they attend school daily. At home, they have a quiet, comfortable place for studying. I make sure they get enough rest and that they eat well-balanced meals. As a parent, watching them grow and being involved with their schoolwork is very satisfying.

After writing your three paragraphs, review them with a classmate. Answer *Yes* or *No* for each question in the space provided. Record your score.

1. Does each paragraph have a topic sentence?

   Paragraph 1 _____ 2 _____ 3 _____

2. Does each paragraph contain at least two sentences in the body?

   Paragraph 1 _____ 2 _____ 3 _____

3. Does the ending sentence tell about the topic?

   Paragraph 1 _____ 2 _____ 3 _____

ACTIVITY 6-2   YOUR GOAL: Get 2 or more answers correct.

The sentences in each of the following paragraphs are not in the correct order. Identify the topic sentence in each. Write the letter *T* in the space provided next to the topic sentence. The first one is completed as an example.

● **WORKING CONDITIONS**

_____ a. In many occupations people usually work regular business hours.

_____ b. They work 40 hours a week, mornings and afternoons.

_____ c. Most people work Monday through Friday.

___T___ d. Working conditions include work hours, the physical environment, and hazards of the job.

_____ e. In other jobs, they may work nights or weekends.

_____ f. Many jobs are in pleasant surroundings; others are in dirty, noisy, or dangerous ones.

_____ g. Working conditions vary and need to be considered before accepting a job.

_____ h. Some jobs require outdoor work.

1. **EARNINGS**

_____ a. Therefore, it is not possible to say that people in one occupation earn more than those in another.

_____ b. They vary depending on the level of responsibility and experience.

_____ c. Earnings also depend on the type of job and geographic location.

_____ d. People working at entry-level jobs do not earn as much as those with more complex jobs.

_____ e. Earnings may vary in different occupations.

_____ f. People in supervisory jobs earn more.

2.   **HIGH BLOOD PRESSURE**

_____ a. High blood pressure is also called *hypertension.*

_____ b. Experts feel that mild hypertension can be controlled through diet and exercise.

_____ c. High blood pressure is one of the most common cardiovascular problems.

_____ d. A statistic from the American Heart Association shows that in 1990, one out of every three adults has high blood pressure.

_____ e. It contributes to the high rate of heart attacks and strokes.

3.   **COUPLE LOSES HOME DUE TO CLERICAL ERROR**

_____ a. Everything from antique furniture to photographs, dishes, and clothes were hauled to a landfill.

_____ b. My aunt and uncle lost all of their possessions because of a clerical error.

_____ c. They were shocked and upset to lose everything.

_____ d. One afternoon a group of movers and a bulldozer appeared at their front door.

_____ e. A clerical error was made; 358 Brown Street, not 348, should have been cleaned out.

_____ f. My aunt and uncle finally found out what happened.

_____ g. They cleaned out and bulldozed the house.

4.   **BUYING A HOME**

_____ a. It is the largest financial investment that will be made.

_____ b. Buying a home is also a major financial responsibility.

_____ c. Buying a home is a major decision for most people.

_____ d. There are many advantages to owning a home.

_____ e. Some advantages include tax savings and equity.

_____ f. Is buying a home a decision you have made or will be making?

☞ *Check your work. Record your score.*

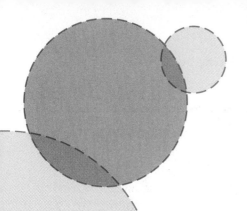

UNIT 7
NOTES AND MESSAGES

WHAT YOU WILL LEARN

When you finish this unit, you will be able to:
- Write short notes.
- Write personal and business telephone messages.

SHORT NOTES AND MESSAGES

We write notes and messages in our personal lives and on the job. Writing a short note or message is sometimes the best way to communicate with people when talking is not practical.

Some of the common notes written are notes to your child's school or notes for a baby-sitter. Other notes are written to family and friends. The most common message written is the telephone message.

Guidelines for Writing Notes and Messages

Most notes and messages are short and contain only one to five sentences. Follow these guidelines when writing notes and messages.

1. Include the name of the person the note or message is for.
2. Include what you want the person to know. What you say should be clear and easy to understand.
3. When writing telephone messages, be sure the details such as name, date, and time are correct.
4. Sign the note or message.
5. Write legibly.
6. Spell all words correctly.
7. Use correct grammar, punctuation, and capitalization.

Different Kinds of Notes

Notes are written in your personal life daily. For instance, you make a checklist of things to do or a grocery list. These are reminder notes usually written to yourself. Other notes are written to family members, friends, businesses, or schools. The following are examples of notes you may have occasion to write.

Example of Note to Family Member to Run Errands:

> July 8
>
> Pete,
> On your way home from work, please pick up the laundry from the cleaners. Also, please shop for these groceries:
> 1/2 gal. milk
> 1 doz. eggs
> 1 loaf wheat bread   Thanks.
> 1/2 gal. vanilla ice cream   Love, Liz

Example of Note for Baby-sitter:

> 3/18
>
> Dora, Spencer should be fed lunch at 11:30 a.m. and dinner at 5:30 p.m. He can have a peanut butter sandwich in the afternoon if he's hungry. In case of an emergency, I can be reached at 555-7896. I'll be home by 8:30 p.m.   Mrs. Nguyen

Example of Note to School for Sick Child:

> 10/21
>
> Dear Mr. Cooper,
> Please excuse Rafael for being absent
> on October 19 and 20. He had the flu and
> is still taking medicine.
>   Sincerely,
>   Mrs. Chacon

Example of Note to Exchange Jacket Ordered by Mail:

> January 12
>
> To Order Department,
> The enclosed jacket is too small. Please
> exchange it for a size 12. Also, instead
> of red, I would like blue.
>   Thank You,
>   Kevin Barrett

✔ **CHECKPOINT 7-1**

YOUR GOAL: Get 20 or more answers correct.

Write the following notes on a blank sheet of paper.

1. Write a note with instructions to a baby-sitter.

2. Write a note to your son asking him to do a household chore when he gets home from school.

3. You ordered an electric coffeepot. The glass decanter arrived with a crack, and the handle was broken. You are returning the glass decanter and would like a replacement. Write a note explaining the problem and what you want.

4. You had a death in the family, which caused your daughter to miss three days of school. Write a note to her school principal, Ms. Walker, explaining why she was absent.

5. Write a note to a family member to shop for cereal, peanut butter, six apples, and popcorn.

Answer the following questions about each of the notes you have written. Put a check mark in the Yes or No space provided for each note.

	1 2 3 4 5	1 2 3 4 5

1. Is the name of the person you are writing to included on the note?   Yes __ __ __ __ __   No __ __ __ __ __

2. Is the date included?   Yes __ __ __ __ __   No __ __ __ __ __

3. Is the note clear and complete?   Yes __ __ __ __ __   No __ __ __ __ __

4. Did you sign the note?   Yes __ __ __ __ __   No __ __ __ __ __

5. Is your handwriting legible?   Yes __ __ __ __ __   No __ __ __ __ __

☞ **Check your work. Record your score.**

TELEPHONE MESSAGES

Messages taken over the telephone may be personal or business messages. A notepad or scrap of paper may be used for a personal telephone message. Usually, a form is used for a business telephone message.

Personal Telephone Messages

Personal telephone messages are usually written for family members. The following are some examples of personal telephone messages.

Example:

> 3/16
>
> Lilly,
> Herb's Camera Shop called.
> Your pictures are ready
> to be picked up.
>   Susan

Example:

> 6/18
>
> Dad,
> Dr. Hasting's nurse
> called to confirm your
> appointment on Tuesday,
> June 20, at 3:30 p.m.
>   Mark

Illustration 7-1 shows a person taking a personal telephone message and a business telephone message.

Illustration 7-1

Writing
Telephone
Messages

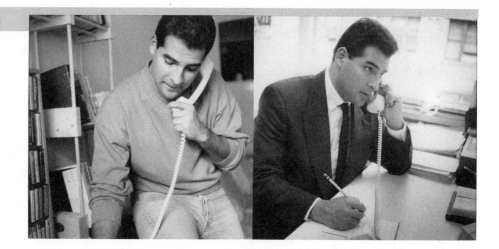

✔ CHECKPOINT 7-2

YOUR GOAL:
Get 2 answers
correct.

Read the information in the following two examples. Put a check mark in the space provided next to the most complete message for each example.

1. Mr. Ruiz received a telephone call for his daughter Celia. Celia was not at home. The call was from Mrs. Nakasone who would like Celia to baby-sit this coming Friday evening. She wants Celia to call her at 555-3363. The call was received on May 22. Mr. Ruiz wrote a message for Celia.

a. _____

> Celia,   5/22
> Can you baby-sit Friday? Call
> 555-3363.
>   Dad

b. _____

> Celia,   5/22
> Mrs. Nakasone would like you to
> baby-sit this Friday evening. Please
> call her at 555-3363 today.
>   Dad

c. _____

> Celia,
> Mrs. Nakasone called. Call her at
> 555-3363.
>   Dad

2. Rudi's Auto Repair called to speak to Sam. Sam is not at home. The mechanic found that the clutch on Sam's car needs to be replaced. Chris, the service manager, needs Sam's okay before they do the work. The shop number is 555-3789. The call to Sam was received on July 14.

a. _____

> July 14
>
> Sam,
> Rudi's Auto Repair called. The clutch on your car needs to be replaced. They need your okay to do the work. Please call Chris, Service Manager, at 555-3789.
> Jean

b. _____

> Sam,
> Please call Chris at Rudi's Auto Repair.
> Jean

c. _____

> July 14
>
> Sam,
> Please call the Auto Shop about your clutch. 555-3789.

☞ *Check your work. Record your score.*

WRITING GEMS—Famous Words from the Past

"But why, some say, the moon? . . . We choose to go to the moon . . . and do the other things, not because they are easy but because they are hard; because that goal will serve to organize and measure the best of our energies and skills . . . the moon and the planets are there, and new hopes for knowledge and peace are there."

John F. Kennedy, 35th U.S. President

Business Telephone Messages

Writing telephone messages is one of the most common forms of communication on the job. Most offices use a standard form for writing telephone messages. The person writing the message completes the form and checks the appropriate boxes. The following message is written on a standard form.

Example:

Mr. Jones called Betty Kang on June 14 at 3:30 P.M. She was out of the office. He has a question about his service agreement. He wants her to return his call at (818) 555-8629. The message was taken by Ron Simms.

For _Betty Kang_

Date _6/14_   Time _3:30p.m._

WHILE YOU WERE OUT

M _Mr. Jones_

From _____

Phone No. _(818)_   _555-8629_

| | Area Code | Number | Extension |

TELEPHONED	✓	**URGENT**	
PLEASE CALL	✓	WANTS TO SEE YOU	
WILL CALL AGAIN		CAME TO SEE YOU	

| RETURNED YOUR CALL | |

Message _He has a question about his service agreement._

Ron Simms

SIGNED

CHECKPOINT 7-3

YOUR GOAL:
Get 4 or more.
answers correct.

Write a business telephone message using the following information. Use the standard form provided.

Message:

Jerry McKenna from National Auto Parts called to speak to Donna Carson. The tires will be delivered tomorrow afternoon. The call was on August 28 at 9:30 A.M. Mr. McKenna's telephone number is 555-7351.

Answer the following questions about your message. Write *Yes* or *No* in the space provided.

1. _____ Is the message dated?

2. _____ Is the time included?

3. _____ Is the box by *telephoned* checked?

4. _____ Is the message complete?

5. _____ Is the message signed?

TELEPHONE MESSAGE

For _____

Date _____ Time _____

WHILE YOU WERE OUT

M _____

From _____

Phone No. _____

         Area Code   Number   Extension

TELEPHONED		**URGENT**	
PLEASE CALL		WANTS TO SEE YOU	
WILL CALL AGAIN		CAME TO SEE YOU	
	RETURNED YOUR CALL		

Message _____

_____

_____

_____

SIGNED

☞ *Check your work. Record your score.*

WHAT YOU HAVE LEARNED

As a result of completing this unit, you have learned to:
- Write short notes and personal and business messages.
- Follow the guidelines for writing notes and messages.

ACTIVITY 7-1   **YOUR GOAL:** Get 4 or more answers correct.

Read each of the following notes and messages. Put a check mark in the space provided that best describes the note or message. The first one is completed as an example.

- **Short Note:**

> Eric,
>   Coach Gonzales called.   11/2
>   Mom

a. _____ The note is written clearly and accurately.

b. ___✓___ The note does not say what the caller wanted.

c. _____ There are misspelled words in the note.

1. **Short Note:**

> Dear Mrs. Davis,   10/2
> Please excuse Marilyn from class.
> She has a dental appointment. I
> will pick her up at 2:30 p.m.
>   Thank You.

a. _____ The note does not tell who it is for.

b. _____ The note is not signed.

c. _____ The note is not clear.

2. **Short Note:**

> 9/15
>
> Scott,
> I'll be home at 7:30 p.m. Please put the chicken in the oven at 6:15 p.m. Bake for one hour at 325°.
>
> Thanks,
> Mom

a. _____ The note does not say who the note is for.

b. _____ The note is not signed.

c. _____ The note is written clearly.

3. **Personal Telephone Message:**

> March 22
>
> Lani,
> Grandmother called. She will be flying on U.S. Airlines, Flight 256 and arrive at 4:45 p.m.
>
> John

a. _____ The message does not tell what day her flight will arrive.

b. _____ The message is not signed.

c. _____ The message does not tell who called.

4. Business Telephone Message:

For _____

Date __5/22_____ Time _2:30 p.m._

WHILE YOU WERE OUT

M _____
From _National Telephone Systems_
Phone No. _(714) 555-5237 35_
    Area Code   Number   Extension

TELEPHONED	✓	URGENT	
PLEASE CALL	✓	WANTS TO SEE YOU	
WILL CALL AGAIN		CAME TO SEE YOU	

RETURNED YOUR CALL | |

Message _Would like to discuss their new long-distance calling service._

_____

_____ _Arden Lindsey_
SIGNED

a. _____ The message does not include a telephone number.

b. _____ The message is not clear.

c. _____ The message does not tell who called.

5. Business Telephone Message:

For _Julie McBride_____

Date _____ Time _9:15 a.m._

WHILE YOU WERE OUT

M _Barry Lau_____
From _The Daily Chronicle_
Phone No. _(808) 555-2183 453_
    Area Code   Number   Extension

TELEPHONED		URGENT	
PLEASE CALL		WANTS TO SEE YOU	
WILL CALL AGAIN		CAME TO SEE YOU	

RETURNED YOUR CALL | |

Message _Has a question about the job ad we are placing in the paper._

_____

_____ _Ann Segura_
SIGNED

a. _____ The message is not dated.

b. _____ The message does not tell who called.

c. _____ The message is not signed.

☞ *Check your work. Record your score.*

ACTIVITY 7-2   YOUR GOAL: Get 12 or more answers correct.

Write a short note, a personal telephone message, and a business telephone message in each of the spaces provided.

1. Write a short note asking a friend to water your plants while you are on vacation.

_____

2. Write a personal telephone message. The message is for your daughter Teri. Debbie called to tell her that softball practice is on Saturday at 2:30 P.M. at Fuller Park. Debbie called on June 23.

3. Write a business telephone message on the standard form provided. Use the following information.

Message:

Gary Bianco from the Graphics Department called on May 14 at 8:30 A.M. The call was for Alicia Gomez. He has a question about the advertisement he is designing. He would like Ms. Gomez to return his call. His extension is 4825.

For _____

Date _____ Time _____

WHILE YOU WERE OUT

M _____

From _____

Phone No. _____
          Area Code   Number   Extension

TELEPHONED		**URGENT**	
PLEASE CALL		WANTS TO SEE YOU	
WILL CALL AGAIN		CAME TO SEE YOU	
	RETURNED YOUR CALL		

Message _____

_____

_____

_____

_____

SIGNED

Answer the following questions about each of the notes and messages you have written. Put a check mark in the Yes or No space provided for each note and message.

		1	2	3		1	2	3
1.	Is the name of the person you are writing to included on the note or message?	Yes ___	___	___	No ___	___	___	
2.	Is the date included?	Yes ___	___	___	No ___	___	___	
3.	Is the note or message clear and complete?	Yes ___	___	___	No ___	___	___	
4.	Did you sign the note?	Yes ___	___	___	No ___	___	___	
5.	Is your handwriting legible?	Yes ___	___	___	No ___	___	___	

☞ *Check your work. Record your score.*

PART THREE
WRITING TO GET A JOB

UNIT 8
A PERSONAL PROFILE

UNIT 9
RESUME

UNIT 10
JOB APPLICATIONS

UNIT 11
PERSONAL/BUSINESS LETTERS

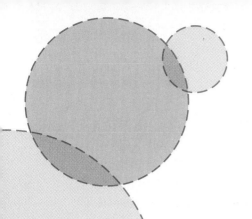

UNIT 8
A PERSONAL PROFILE

WHAT YOU WILL LEARN

When you finish this unit, you will be able to:
- Complete the first step in marketing your talents.
- Identify the parts of a Personal Profile.
- Develop an up-to-date Personal Profile for yourself.

MARKETING YOUR TALENTS

Marketing your talents is a six-step process for getting a job. The first step in marketing your talents is to look at what your qualifications are. You will need to write a detailed Personal Profile of your background. This profile will include your education and job experience. A Personal Profile will help you know what you have to offer an employer. The Personal Profile is for your own use. Do not send or give it to an employer. You will use it as a personal resource when you apply for a job.

The Personal Profile will give you an up-to-date written history of yourself. All the information about yourself will be organized and written in one place. As your experience changes, you will keep your Personal Profile updated.

The second step in marketing your talents is to prepare a resume. Resume preparation is presented in Unit 9.

The third step is to complete an application for a job. Job applications are presented in Unit 10.

The fourth step is to send a letter of application and resume to an employer. Letters of application are discussed in Unit 11.

The fifth step is the job interview. A job interview is your showcase for marketing your talents. During the interview, the employer judges your qualifications.

The sixth and last step is the job interview follow-up. Writing a follow-up letter is presented in Unit 11.

PARTS OF A PERSONAL PROFILE

Your Personal Profile will contain different types of information about yourself. In this unit, each section of the Personal Profile will be described. An example will be presented, and you will be asked to write this information about yourself. If you have access to a computer, you could key this information as it is presented.

Personal Information

Personal information includes your name, current address, telephone number, Social Security number, date of birth, and driver's license number.

Example:

> Pat Sousa McClain
> 5235 Sky Ridge Avenue; Sacramento, CA 95818-4567
> (916) 555-4182 SS No. 536-58-6312
> Date of Birth—May 24, 1955 Driver's License No. B036 1533

CHECKPOINT 8-1

YOUR GOAL:
Get 5 or more points.

Write your personal information on a blank sheet of paper. Title this section *Personal Information*.

☞ *Check your work. Record your score.*

Educational Background

List the schools you attended—high school, trade or technical school, community college, or other special schools. Include the addresses and dates you attended.

Example:

> Luther Burbank High School
>   3500 Florin Road; Sacramento, CA 95823-3456 1969–1974
> Sacramento Vocational Center, Restaurant Program
>   9738 Lincoln Ave.; Sacramento, CA 95827-2313 1981–1982
> American College
>   4700 College Dr.; Sacramento, CA 95841-1234 1984–1986

GETTING READY TO GO TO WORK—Preparing for the Job Interview

- Learn about the company or business.
- Have a specific job or jobs in mind.
- Be on time—arrive a few minutes early.
- Prepare to answer questions about yourself and previous jobs.

CHECKPOINT 8-2

YOUR GOAL:
Get 3 or more points.

Write your educational background on a blank sheet of paper. Title this section *Educational Background*.

☞ *Check your work. Record your score.*

Specialized Courses and Certificates

What specialized courses did you take in school? When did you take them? List any certificates you received. Two specialized course classrooms are shown in Illustration 8-1.

Illustration 8-1

Specialized Courses

Example:

Luther Burbank High School
    Auto Mechanics (1971), Computer Applications (1972),
    Electronics (1973), Accounting (1973–74)

Sacramento Vocational Center, Restaurant Program
    Certificate of Completion (1982)

American College, Spanish I and II (1984–85)
    Restaurant Management (1986)

✔ CHECKPOINT 8-3

YOUR GOAL:
Get 3 or more points.

Write any specialized courses you have taken on a blank sheet of paper. Also list any certificates you have received. Title this section *Specialized Courses and Certificates*.

☞ *Check your work. Record your score.*

Extracurricular Activities and Organizations

While in school, did you belong to any student organizations or groups? Did you play any sports, work on the school paper, or play in the band? Since you left school, have you been a member of any professional organization?

Example:

Future Business Leaders of America (FBLA)—1973–1974
FBLA Vice President—1974   Tennis Team—1972–1974
California Restaurant Association—1984–Present

CHECKPOINT 8-4

YOUR GOAL:
Get 1 point for each item.

Write any extracurricular activities and organizations you were or are now involved in on a blank sheet of paper. Title this section *Extracurricular Activities and Organizations*.

☞ *Check your work. Record your score.*

Honors and Awards

What honors and awards have you received?

Example:

FBLA State Accounting Competition, First Place, 1974

Most Valuable Player Tennis Award, 1973

Spring Fair, Salad-Making Competition, Second Place, 1982

CHECKPOINT 8-5

YOUR GOAL:
Get 1 point for each item.

Write your honors and awards on a blank sheet of paper. Title this section *Honors and Awards*.

☞ *Check your work. Record your score.*

Work History

List all of your jobs including part-time, summer, and volunteer work. Give the name and address of each of your employers, job title or job duties, and supervisor. Include the dates you worked and the starting and final salary you earned. Give your reason for leaving the job. Your most recent or current job will be the last one on your list.

Example:

Sacramento Christian Church, 435 Watt Ave., Sacramento, CA 95823-1234;
    Child Care Volunteer—11/69–8/71
Job Title: Child Care Assistant
Supervisor: Mr. John Tinsley—(916) 555-2754

McDonald's, 3756 Arden Way, Sacramento, CA 95823-3254
Job Title: Fry Cook, Cashier—9/71–9/74
Supervisor: Mrs. Leah Gomez—(916) 555-5689
Starting Salary: $1.75 per hour Final: $2.00 per hour
Part-time job. Left for job at Bob's Restaurant

Bob's Restaurant, 375 16th Street, Sacramento, CA 95818-6234
Job Title: Restaurant Pastry Chef—10/74–2/82
Supervisor: Mr. George Clark—(916) 555-7451
Starting Salary: $5.00 per hour Final: $8.50 per hour
Left for job at Madison Grill

Madison Grill, 263 Madison, Sacramento, CA 95823-7139
Job Title: Assistant Kitchen Manager. Promoted to
Kitchen Manager in 1984. Supervise eight employees. 3/82–Present
Supervisor: Ms. Julia Goldstein—(916) 555-8903
Starting Salary: $21,000 Current Salary: $26,500

CHECKPOINT 8-6

YOUR GOAL:
Get 1 point for each item.

Write all the information about your past employment on a blank sheet of paper. Title this section *Work History*.

☞ *Check your work. Record your score.*

Skills and Abilities

Do you have special skills? What do you do well? Do you operate any special type of equipment? Do you speak, read, or write another language other than English?

Example:

> Good at details; excellent organizational skills. Like working with people. Ten-Key Calculator and Macintosh Computer, Excel and Microsoft Word software. Speak, read, and write Spanish fluently.

CHECKPOINT 8-7

YOUR GOAL:
Get 2 or more points.

Write your skills and abilities on a blank sheet of paper. Title this section *Skills and Abilities*.

☞ *Check your work. Record your score.*

Interests, Talents, and Aptitudes

What are your special interests, talents, and aptitudes? What are your hobbies?

Example:

> Good with figures. Like math and accounting.
>
> Hobbies: Reading, fishing, playing tennis, and karate.

CHECKPOINT 8-8

YOUR GOAL:
Get 2 or more points.

Write your talents, interests, and aptitudes on a blank sheet of paper. Title this section *Interests, Talents, and Aptitudes*.

☞ *Check your work. Record your score.*

Career Objective

What kind of job do you want? List the types of jobs you feel best qualified for. What is your career goal? Possible job titles are shown in Illustration 8-2.

Illustration 8-2

Career Options—What Is Your Goal?

Example:

Qualified for: Chef, Kitchen Manager
Career Objective: Restaurant Manager

CHECKPOINT 8-9

YOUR GOAL:
Get 2 or more points.

Write the jobs you are qualified for on a blank sheet of paper. Also write down your future career goal. Title this section *Career Objective.*

☞ *Check your work. Record your score.*

GETTING READY TO GO TO WORK—Personal Appearance for the Interview

● Be well groomed.
● Dress appropriately.
● Do not chew gum or smoke.

References

Most jobs require references. References are people who can say that you are a good worker. Ask permission before using a person's name as a reference. List former employers, instructors, or other people who can write a positive letter or answer questions about you. Do not use names of relatives. Include names, addresses, and telephone numbers.

Example:

Ms. Rita Chastain, Instructor
Restaurant Program, Sacramento Vocational Center
9738 Lincoln Ave.
Sacramento, CA 95827-2313
(916) 555-6648

Mr. George Clark, Kitchen Manager
Bob's Restaurant
375 16th Street
Sacramento, CA 95818-6234
(916) 555-7451

Ms. Julia Goldstein, Owner
Madison Grill
263 Madison
Sacramento, CA 95823-7139
(916) 555-8903

✔ CHECKPOINT 8-10

YOUR GOAL:
Get 3 or more points.

Write three references on a blank sheet of paper. Title this section *References*.

☞ *Check your work. Record your score.*

WHAT YOU HAVE LEARNED

As a result of completing this unit, you have learned that:

- A Personal Profile is a step toward marketing your talents.
- A Personal Profile includes—personal information; educational background; work history; skills and abilities; interests, talents, and aptitudes; career objective; and references.
- A completed Personal Profile is an up-to-date written history about yourself.

ACTIVITY 8-1   YOUR GOAL: Get 5 or more answers correct.

Match the information in the left column with one of the Personal Profile steps in the right column. Write the correct letter in each of the spaces provided. The first one is completed as an example.

- ___c___ Mr. A. T. Herrera, Counselor
  Alhambra Technical School
  487 Oak Drive
  Columbus, OH 43210-5487
  (614) 555-9854

1. _____ Lang's Foreign Car Garage
   487 Sierra Avenue
   Bloomington, IN 47402-4891
   Job Title: Mechanic
   8/89–Present
   Supervisor: Ted Lang
   Salary: $11.50 per hour

2. _____ Speak and write Spanish

3. _____ Bank Teller Program,
   Received Certificate of
   Completion, 1989

4. _____ Licensed Practical Nurse

5. _____ Washington Adult School
   458 West Street
   Boise, ID 83720-4587
   1986–1987

6. _____ Photography, cooking,
   and oil painting

7. _____ Doris Chung, Vice President
   First Western Bank
   3486 Foothill Blvd.
   Houston, TX 77224-9532
   (713) 555-5211

a. Career Objective

b. Educational Background

c. References

d. Skills and Abilities

e. Specialized Courses and
   Certificates

f. Interests, Talents, and
   Aptitudes

g. Work History

☞ *Check your work. Record your score.*

UNIT 9
RESUME

WHAT YOU WILL LEARN

When you finish this unit, you will be able to:
- Understand the purpose of a resume.
- Follow guidelines for preparing a resume.
- Develop a resume using a resume format and outline.
- Practice using resume language.

PURPOSE OF A RESUME

A **resume** is a summary of a person's background and qualifications. The purpose of a resume is to show an employer that a job applicant has the experience or education for the position. The resume lists the applicant's personal information, employment objective, education, work history, special skills, and references. A resume is sometimes called a *data sheet.*

Many jobs you apply for will require a resume. An effective resume "gets your foot in the door." It often leads to job interviews that you might not otherwise have.

CHECKPOINT 9-1

YOUR GOAL:
Get 4 or more answers correct.

Each of the following statements about the resume is either true or false. Write *True* in the space provided beside each true statement. Write *False* in the space provided beside each false statement. The first one is completed as an example.

___True___ • A resume is sometimes called a data sheet.

_____ 1. All jobs require a resume.

_____ 2. A resume includes work history and references.

112

_____   3. A resume is a summary of a job applicant's background and qualifications.

_____   4. A resume guarantees you an interview.

_____   5. Education is not listed on a resume.

☞ *Check your work. Record your score.*

GUIDELINES FOR WRITING A RESUME

A resume should summarize your qualifications and work history. The Personal Profile developed in Unit 8 will provide most of the information needed for writing your resume. The resume does not include everything that is on a Personal Profile. When you prepare your resume, follow these guidelines:

1. Keep your resume brief. Limit your resume to two pages.
2. Key your resume; never hand print.
3. Use a format that is readable and attractive in appearance. Leave white space on both sides, top, and bottom of the page.
4. Use good quality white paper.
5. Proofread carefully for correct spelling and punctuation.
6. Make neat corrections if you make any errors in keying.

RESUME FORMATS

There is no perfect resume format. The key is to present information that is brief, but complete. The resume should be attractive, neat, and easy to read. Two resume formats are used in this unit. Both formats use most of the information in the Personal Profile prepared in Unit 8. Look at the two different kinds of resumes shown in Illustration 9-1 and Illustration 9-2.

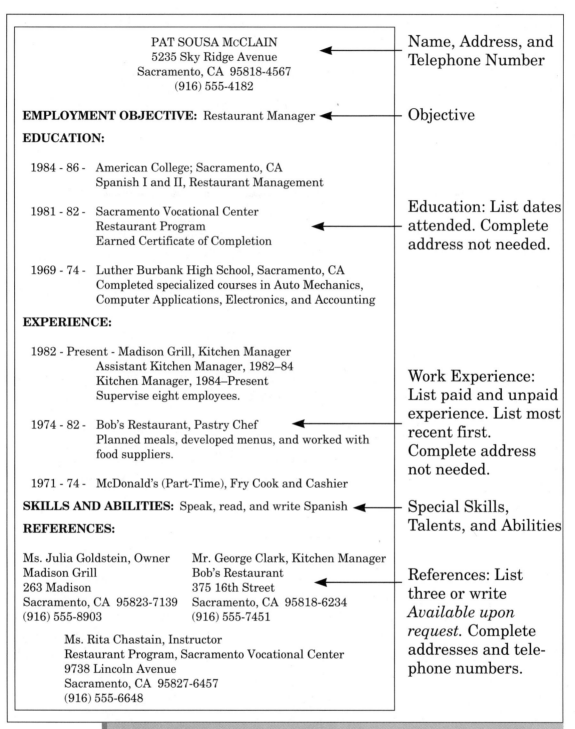

PAT SOUSA McCLAIN
5235 Sky Ridge Avenue
Sacramento, CA 95818-4567
(916) 555-4182   ◄──── Name, Address, and
                                                  Telephone Number

EMPLOYMENT OBJECTIVE: Restaurant Manager ◄──── Objective

EDUCATION:

1984 - 86 - American College; Sacramento, CA
            Spanish I and II, Restaurant Management

1981 - 82 - Sacramento Vocational Center
            Restaurant Program   ◄──── Education: List dates
            Earned Certificate of Completion   attended. Complete
                                                 address not needed.

1969 - 74 - Luther Burbank High School, Sacramento, CA
            Completed specialized courses in Auto Mechanics,
            Computer Applications, Electronics, and Accounting

EXPERIENCE:

1982 - Present - Madison Grill, Kitchen Manager
            Assistant Kitchen Manager, 1982–84
            Kitchen Manager, 1984–Present   Work Experience:
            Supervise eight employees.   List paid and unpaid
                                                 experience. List most
1974 - 82 - Bob's Restaurant, Pastry Chef ◄──── recent first.
            Planned meals, developed menus, and worked with Complete address
            food suppliers.   not needed.

1971 - 74 - McDonald's (Part-Time), Fry Cook and Cashier

SKILLS AND ABILITIES: Speak, read, and write Spanish ◄──── Special Skills,
                                                              Talents, and Abilities

REFERENCES:

Ms. Julia Goldstein, Owner   Mr. George Clark, Kitchen Manager
Madison Grill   Bob's Restaurant   References: List
263 Madison   375 16th Street   three or write
Sacramento, CA 95823-7139   Sacramento, CA 95818-6234 ◄────   *Available upon
(916) 555-8903   (916) 555-7451   request.* Complete
                                                                addresses and tele-
    Ms. Rita Chastain, Instructor   phone numbers.
    Restaurant Program, Sacramento Vocational Center
    9738 Lincoln Avenue
    Sacramento, CA 95827-6457
    (916) 555-6648

Illustration 9-1

Example Resume with Side Headings

LEE GUZMAN ROMERO

5987 Galisteo Dr.   Phone: (505) 555-4631
Santa Fe, NM 87504-3165   Evenings: After 5:30 p.m.

CAREER OBJECTIVE

Licensed Practical Nurse (LPN)

EDUCATION

Santa Fe Community College - Currently enrolled in Registered Nursing Program.   Have completed 24 semester units.

Voc-Tech Skills Center, Santa Fe. Completed Licensed Practical Nurse Program in 1990. Received State Certification, July 1990.

Engeneria High School, Guadalajara, Mexico, 1982 - 1986. Completed Nurse Assistant Program.

WORK HISTORY

Guadalajara Nursing Center   -   Certified Nurse Assistant
Guadalajara, Mexico   July 1986–August 1987

Delgado Convalescent Home   -   Certified Nurse Assistant
Santa Fe, New Mexico   November 1987 - June 1989

SPECIAL SKILLS

Spanish - Speak, read, and write.
Experience in home care, nursing homes, and hospitals.

REFERENCES

Available upon request.

Illustration 9-2

Example Resume with Centered Headings

GETTING READY TO GO TO WORK—Where to Find Out About Job Openings

- State Employment Offices
- Employers
- Civil Service Announcements
- Employment Agencies
- Newspaper Classified Ads
- School Placement Services
- Libraries
- Community Centers
- Labor Unions
- Friends and Relatives

RESUME OUTLINE

The example resumes in this unit show two commonly used formats. Each resume has similar basic information about the applicant. Study the following outline for developing your resume:

1. Personal Information
2. Career or Employment Objective
3. Education
4. Work History or Experience
5. Special Skills and Abilities
6. References

To complete the following Checkpoints, follow the format presented in Illustration 9-1 using side headings. Use the Personal Profile you developed in Unit 8 as a resource. Write the information on a blank sheet of paper.

✓ CHECKPOINT 9-2

YOUR GOAL:
Get one point for each correct item.

Write your Personal Information. Put your name, address, and telephone number at the top of the page. Don't list weight, height, or date of birth.

☞ *Check your work. Record your score.*

CHECKPOINT 9-3

YOUR GOAL:
Get 1 point.

Write your Career Objective. Title this section *Career Objective* or *Objective*. If there is a specific job you are applying for, list this job.

☞ *Check your work. Record your score.*

CHECKPOINT 9-4

YOUR GOAL:
Get 10 points.

Write information about your educational background. Title this section *Education*. Include school names, addresses, dates of attendance, degrees, and certificates received.

☞ *Check your work. Record your score.*

CHECKPOINT 9-5

YOUR GOAL:
Get 10 points.

Write your work history—paid and volunteer work. Title this section *Work History* or *Experience*. Include the following for each job: job title, name and address of employer, and dates of employment. Begin with the most recent experience. Do not include salary information on a resume. This information goes on the job application—the next step.

☞ *Check your work. Record your score.*

CHECKPOINT 9-6

YOUR GOAL:
Get 1 point for each item.

Write your special skills and abilities. Include any special equipment and machines you can operate. Title this section *Special Skills*.

☞ *Check your work. Record your score.*

CHECKPOINT 9-7

YOUR GOAL:
Get 10 points.

References can be included on a resume. Another option is to note on your resume that your references are "available upon request." List the names, addresses, and telephone numbers of three references you could include. Title this section *References*.

☞ *Check your work. Record your score.*

RESUME LANGUAGE

Resume language is brief and to the point. A resume should be no longer than two pages.

To make your resume easy to read, use short, simple words. Complete sentences are not necessary. Resume writing is mastering the skill of saying a lot in a small amount of space. The following example is wordy:

> In 1990, after two years of experience as a salesclerk, I decided it was time to seek more responsibility. I applied for and received a promotion from salesclerk to sales manager in January.

Here is a brief version of the same paragraph:

Salesclerk 1988 - 90; Sales Manager 1990 - Present

In listing your skills, talents, and accomplishments, use words that describe. Words such as *organized, directed, supervised, operated,* and *designed* emphasize your job duties. Remember, you are trying to make an impression on the employer. You want to catch the employer's attention.

CHECKPOINT 9-8

YOUR GOAL:
Get 5 points.

Write the following information in resume language in the spaces provided:

1. Attended the Automotive Technical Institute in Detroit, Michigan, for two years. Completed the program and graduated in 1989. Received Automotive Mechanic Certificate.

_____

_____

_____

2. Worked as an Auto Mechanic Assistant for one year. It was a full-time job at Yee's Foreign Car Repair from August 1986 to August 1987. The shop is located in Lansing, Michigan.

_____

_____

_____

☞ *Check your work. Record your score.*

WHAT YOU HAVE LEARNED

As a result of completing this unit, you have learned that:
- A resume is needed for some jobs.
- Guidelines should be followed when preparing a resume.
- There is a standard resume format and outline.
- Resume language is brief and to the point.

ACTIVITY 9-1   **YOUR GOAL:** Get 5 or more answers correct.

The following sections are included in a resume: Education, References, Personal Information, Skills and Abilities, Objective, and Experience. Write the order in which they should appear in a resume in the spaces provided.

1. _____

2. _____

3. _____

4. _____

5. _____

6. _____

☞ *Check your work. Record your score.*

ACTIVITY 9-2   **YOUR GOAL:** Get 10 or more answers correct.

Underline the errors in the following resume information:

EDUCATION:

1. 1988 - 1990 - Tulsa County Area vocational School
             Tulsa, oklahoma
             Completed Building construction Prgram

REFERENCES:

2. Ms. Lydia Hill, Managr
   Hill's Building emporium
   3454 Main Stret
   Portland, or 97204-2101
   555-9479

3. mr. Gene osaki, Instructor
   Carpenter's apprenticeship Program
   458 Broadway, suite C
   eugene, OR 97405-6584
   (503) 555-396

☞ *Check your work. Record your score.*

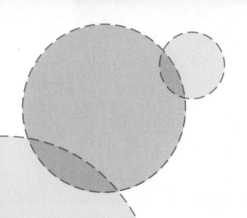

UNIT 10
JOB APPLICATIONS

WHAT YOU WILL LEARN

When you finish this unit, you will be able to:
- Understand why employers use job applications.
- Complete different parts of a job application.

PURPOSE OF JOB APPLICATIONS

For most jobs, employers will ask you to fill out an application form. You will list the schools you have attended and any special training you have had. You will also list work experience and your references. Other information is also asked for on the form. Your completed job application tells about your qualifications. It helps an employer decide whether you should be given a job interview.

You will sometimes be asked to complete the job application at the place of business. In most cases, you can take the job application to complete at home.

How you complete the application shows the employer how well you can understand and follow instructions. It also shows the employer how neat you are. A sloppy application with errors may mean you cannot perform a simple job. Each business has its own job application form. Therefore, you need to read and follow instructions carefully.

The job application is usually the first thing an employer sees about you. You will want to make a good first impression. Study these tips on completing job applications.

1. Print the application in ink or key it. If you key the application, the keying should be slightly above the lines. Be as neat as possible.
2. Make sure your address is complete. The ZIP Code is part of your address.

3. Answer every question that applies to you. If a question does not apply, write *NA,* which means *not applicable.* NA tells the employer you did not skip answering the question.

4. Write the city and state where you were born under Place of Birth. Include the country if you were not born in the United States.

5. Take your Personal Profile with you. This information will be handy should you have to complete the job application at the business site.

6. Proofread your application. Be sure to spell correctly. The employer expects your application to show YOUR BEST WORK. Create a good impression.

7. Make a photocopy of your completed job application, if possible. You can use it as a quick guide when you have to complete other applications.

GETTING READY TO GO TO WORK—Verification of Your Right to Work

When you are hired for a job, you must furnish your Social Security card and one of the following documents within 72 hours of starting work:

- a card issued by federal, state, or local government showing your identity;
- U.S. military card or other draft card;
- driver's license or state-issued I.D. card with photo;
- school I.D. card with photo;
- U.S. passport;
- voter's registration card; or
- current Immigration and Naturalization Service (INS) forms with employment authorization stamp.

COMPLETING JOB APPLICATIONS

Job applications are usually two to four pages long. Most applications ask for the same information. The format of the job application will vary.

The following are examples of the most common questions asked on job applications. The Personal Profile in Unit 8 for Pat Sousa McClain was used in the following examples. Your Personal Profile will help you in completing the Checkpoint exercises in this unit.

Personal Information

The first section of a job application asks for your personal information. The information needed for this section includes name, address, telephone number, and Social Security number.

Example:

APPLICATION FOR EMPLOYMENT
(PLEASE PRINT PLAINLY)

The Civil Rights Act of 1964 prohibits discrimination in employment because of race, color, religion, or national origin. Public Law 90-202 prohibits discrimination because of age. The laws of some states prohibit some or all of the above mentioned types of discrimination.

Last Name	First Name	Middle Initial
McClain	Pat	S.

Apt.	Number and Street	City
	5235 Sky Ridge Avenue	Sacramento

State	Zip Code	Can you, after employment, submit verification of your legal right to work in the United States?
CA	95818-4567	Yes

Are you over 18 years of age?	☒ Yes ☐ No	Telephone Number (include area code)	Social Security Number
		(916) 555-4182	536-58-6312

CHECKPOINT 10-1

YOUR GOAL: Get 4 or more answers correct.

Complete the application form with information about yourself. Read the instructions carefully. Use an ink pen.

APPLICATION FOR EMPLOYMENT
(PLEASE PRINT PLAINLY)

The Civil Rights Act of 1964 prohibits discrimination in employment because of race, color, religion, or national origin. Public Law 90-202 prohibits discrimination because of age. The laws of some states prohibit some or all of the above mentioned types of discrimination.

Last Name	First Name	Middle Initial

Apt.	Number and Street	City	

State	Zip Code	Can you, after employment, submit verification of your legal right to work in the United States?

Are you over 18 years of age? ☐ Yes ☐ No	Telephone Number (include area code)	Social Security Number

☞ **Check your work. Record your score.**

Employment Desired

This section of a job application asks what job you are applying for. If you are interested in more than one job, list them. If there is a specific date you can begin work, write this in. It is appropriate to indicate an hourly wage, such as $7 an hour. An annual salary amount can also be written in. Be realistic on the salary you are asking for.

Many jobs are in the evening and on weekends. Many businesses are open seven days a week. Employers will want to know what you prefer and when you are available to work. Some jobs may be full-time or part-time. In the following example, *no restrictions* means that you can work anytime and any day of the week.

Example:

		Date You Can Start	Salary Desired
Position Applying For: **Restaurant Manager**		**Immediately**	**$ 27,000**

Please check preferred schedule:
☐ I am available and desire to work FULL-TIME and do not have restrictions on my hours and days. (Complete Section B)
☐ I am available and desire PART-TIME work each week. (Complete Section A & B)

A I am only available for PART-TIME because
    ☐ Student   ☐ Other Job   ☐ Other (explain) _____

B Hours Available

	Monday	Tuesday	Wednesday	Thursday	Friday	Saturday	Sunday
"x" if no restrictions	X	X	X	X	X		
I am available to work from	___ to ___	___ to ___	___ to ___	___ to ___	___ to ___	*8a.m.* to *5p.m.*	*8a.m.* to *5p.m.*

✔ CHECKPOINT 10-2

YOUR GOAL:
Get 2 answers correct.

Complete the Employment Desired section of the application form. Think of a job to apply for or pick one of these positions:

- Auto Mechanic
- Legal Secretary
- Salesperson
- Electronics Assembler
- Teacher's Aide
- Dental Assistant
- Nurse
- Bus Driver
- Mail Carrier

		Date You Can Start	Salary Desired
Position Applying For:			

Please check preferred schedule:
☐ I am available and desire to work FULL-TIME and do not have restrictions on my hours and days. (Complete Section B)
☐ I am available and desire PART-TIME work each week. (Complete Section A & B)

A I am only available for PART-TIME because
    ☐ Student   ☐ Other Job   ☐ Other (explain) _____

B Hours Available

	Monday	Tuesday	Wednesday	Thursday	Friday	Saturday	Sunday
"x" if no restrictions							
I am available to work from	___ to ___	___ to ___	___ to ___	___ to ___	___ to ___	___ to ___	___ to ___

☞ *Check your work. Record your score.*

Education ━━━━━━━━━━━━━━━━━━━━━

The Education section of a job application asks about your schooling and training. Some applications will ask the highest grade you completed and the areas you studied. Some applications will ask for any special skills, such as speaking a foreign language, or any special equipment you can operate. If you have any certificates or any licenses, some applications ask for this information.

Example:

		Graduate?
HIGH SCHOOL	*Name* Luther Burbank High School *Address* 3500 Florin Rd., Sacramento, CA 95823-3456	☒ Yes ☐ No
COLLEGE	*Name* American College *Address* 4700 College Dr., Sacramento, CA 95841-1234	☐ Yes ☒ No
OTHER	*Name* Sacramento Vocational Center *Received Certificate* *Address* 9738 Lincoln Ave., Sacramento, CA 95827-2313	☒ Yes ☐ No

✔ ## CHECKPOINT 10-3

YOUR GOAL:
Get 2 answers correct.

Complete this section on Education with information about your schooling.

		Graduate?
HIGH SCHOOL	*Name* _____ *Address* _____	☐ Yes ☐ No
COLLEGE	*Name* _____ *Address* _____	☐ Yes ☐ No
OTHER	*Name* _____ *Address* _____	☐ Yes ☐ No

☞ *Check your work. Record your score.*

Employment Record

The Employment Record section of a job application tells about your work history. If you have not had paid work experience, include volunteer work. Many applications will ask about previous salary earned, reason for leaving a job, and the duties of your different positions held. Most applications will ask you to begin with the most recent job experience.

Example:

Employment Record *All information including salary will be verified*	LIST PRESENT AND PREVIOUS POSITIONS AND VOLUNTEER WORK, STARTING WITH THE MOST RECENT POSITION.

Present or last employer Madison Grill — **Dates (mo./yr.)** From 3/82 To Present — **Current or last position** Kitchen Manager — **Salary (start/final)** $21,000-$26,500

Address 263 Madison; Sacramento, CA 95823-7139 — **Telephone** (916)555-8903

Duties Responsible for operation of the kitchen. Develop daily menus and order supplies. Supervise eight kitchen employees. — **Reason for leaving** —

Previous employer Bob's Restaurant — **Dates (mo./yr.)** From 10/74 To 2/82 — **Current or last position** Restaurant Pastry Chef — **Salary (start/final)** $5-$8.50

Address 375 16th Street; Sacramento, CA 95818-6234 — **Telephone** (916)555-7451

Duties Prepared desserts and bread items. — **Reason for leaving** Job at Madison Grill

Previous employer McDonald's — **Dates (mo./yr.)** From 9/71 To 9/74 — **Current or last position** Part-Time Fry Cook — **Salary (start/final)** $1.75-$2

Address 3756 Arden Way; Sacramento, CA 95823-3254 — **Telephone** (916)555-5689

Duties Grilled hamburgers, prepared sandwiches and salads. — **Reason for leaving** Full-Time job at Bob's Restaurant

Previous employer Sacramento Christian Church — **Dates (mo./yr.)** From 11/69 To 8/71 — **Current or last position** Child Care Assistant — **Salary (start/final)** Volunteer

Address 435 Watt Avenue; Sacramento, CA 95823-1234 — **Telephone** (916)555-2754

Duties Took care of small children while parents attended Sunday church service. — **Reason for leaving** Wanted a paying job.

CHECKPOINT 10-4

YOUR GOAL:
Get 7 or more
answers correct.

Complete the Employment Record of the job application with your work experience. If you have worked outside the United States, be sure to include this experience. Read the questions carefully.

Employment Record
All information including salary will be verified

LIST PRESENT AND PREVIOUS POSITIONS AND VOLUNTEER WORK, STARTING WITH THE MOST RECENT POSITION.

Present or last employer	Dates (mo./yr.) From To	Current or last position	Salary (start/final)
Address			Telephone
Duties		Reason for leaving	

Previous employer	Dates (mo./yr.) From To	Current or last position	Salary (start/final)
Address			Telephone
Duties		Reason for leaving	

Previous employer	Dates (mo./yr.) From To	Current or last position	Salary (start/final)
Address			Telephone
Duties		Reason for leaving	

Previous employer	Dates (mo./yr.) From To	Current or last position	Salary (start/final)
Address			Telephone
Duties		Reason for leaving	

☞ *Check your work. Record your score.*

References

Employers want to know about your character, work habits, and abilities. If you are a recent graduate, you can list instructors who know your schoolwork. Be sure you have the permission of the persons you use as references. You should include only those persons who can give you a good recommendation.

Example:

REFERENCES		
Give names of two persons, not relatives or former employers who have known you for five years or more, that we may contact.		
NAME	ADDRESS	TELEPHONE
Ms. Rita Chastain, Instructor Restaurant Program	9738 Lincoln Avenue Sacramento, CA 95827-2313	(916) 555-6648
Mr. George Clark, Kitchen Bob's Restaurant Manager	375 16th Street Sacramento, CA 95818-6234	(916) 555-7451
Ms. Julia Goldstein, Owner Madison Grill	263 Madison Sacramento, CA 95823-7139	(916) 555-8903

CHECKPOINT 10-5

YOUR GOAL:
Get 3 answers correct.

Complete the References section of the job application.

REFERENCES		
Give names of two persons, not relatives or former employers who have known you for five years or more, that we may contact.		
NAME	ADDRESS	TELEPHONE

☞ *Check your work. Record your score.*

Signature ━━━━━━━━━━━━━━━━━

All applications require your signature. By signing the application, you are verifying that everything you have said is true. Should you falsify anything on the application, you could lose your job.

Example:

> **THIS APPLICATION IS NOT COMPLETE UNTIL THE FOLLOWING STATEMENT IS READ AND SIGNED.**
>
> I certify all the information furnished on this form is true. IF EMPLOYED, I understand that any falsification of this application may be cause for immediate dismissal.
>
> Signed _*Pat Sousa McClain*_____ Date _*7/30/--*_____

CHECKPOINT 10-6

YOUR GOAL:
Get 2 answers correct.

Sign and date the Signature section of the application.

> **THIS APPLICATION IS NOT COMPLETE UNTIL THE FOLLOWING STATEMENT IS READ AND SIGNED.**
>
> I certify all the information furnished on this form is true. IF EMPLOYED, I understand that any falsification of this application may be cause for immediate dismissal.
>
> Signed _____ Date _____

☞ *Check your work. Record your score.*

Other Information on Applications ━━━━━━

You may be asked about any military service you have had. An employer will want to know if you have physical disabilities that may prevent you from performing certain types of jobs. Questions may be asked about any record of criminal convictions.

Many companies test all new employees for drug use. A list of prescription and over-the-counter medications may be requested.

GETTING READY TO GO TO WORK—Questions Asked During Interviews

- Why do you want to work for this company?
- What are your present job responsibilities?
- What do you do best?
- Why do you think you can handle this job?
- What are your future career plans?
- What are your hobbies and interests?
- What questions do you have about the job or our company?
- Why should you be hired for the job?

WHAT YOU HAVE LEARNED

As a result of completing this unit, you have learned:

- Why employers use job applications.
- The different types of questions asked on job applications.
- How to complete a job application.

ACTIVITY 10-1   **YOUR GOAL:** Get 8 or more answers correct.

1. Read the personal information on the following section of a job application. Put a check mark in the space provided next to the statements that are correct.

Last Name Romero		First Name Lee		Middle Initial G.
Apt.	Number and Street 5987 Galisteo Drive		City Santa Fe	
State	Zip Code 87504-6978	Can you, after employment, submit verification of your legal right to work in the United States?		
Are you over 18 years of age?	☒ Yes ☐ No	Telephone Number (include area code) (505) 555-4631		Social Security Number

_____ a. Last and first names are included.

_____ b. The state is included.

_____ c. Area code is included with the telephone number.

_____ d. A Social Security number is included.

2. Read the following education information. Put a check mark in the space provided next to the statements that are correct.

	Name	Graduate?
HIGH SCHOOL	Engeneria High Schol Address	☒ Yes ☐ No
TRADE SCHOOL	Vocational Technical Skils Center Address	☒ Yes ☐ No

_____ a. Addresses are included.

_____ b. Information is written legibly.

_____ c. All words are spelled correctly.

_____ d. Yes or No boxes are marked.

3. Read the following employment information. Put a check mark in the
    space provided next to the statements that are correct.

Previous employer **Delgado Convalescent Home**	Dates (mo./yr.) From **11/87** To **6/90**	Current or last position **Certified Nurse Assistant**	Salary (start/final)
Address **428 Richards Drive ; Santa Fe, NM 87504-4823**			Telephone **(505)555-6133**
Duties **Served meals, fed patients, made beds, bathed patients, completed patient charts.**		Reason for leaving **Job at St. John's Hospital**	

_____ a. Dates include month and year.

_____ b. Salary is included.

_____ c. Telephone number is included.

_____ d. Duties are included.

4. Read the following reference information. Put a check mark in the space
    provided next to the statements that are correct.

REFERENCES		
Give names of two persons, not relatives or former employers who have known you for five years or more, that we may contact.		
NAME	ADDRESS	TELEPHONE
Maria Donovan, Director of Nursing ; St. John's Hospital	428 St. Michaels Drive Santa Fe, NM 87504-6742	
Dr. Alex Reyes Delgado Convalescent Home	428 Richards Drive Santa Fe, NM 87504-4823	

_____ a. Two references are given.

_____ b. Addresses include ZIP Codes.

_____ c. All words are spelled correctly.

_____ d. Telephone numbers are included.

☞ *Check your work. Record your score.*

UNIT 11
PERSONAL/BUSINESS LETTERS

WHAT YOU WILL LEARN

When you finish this unit, you will be able to:
- Write letters of application.
- Write interview follow-up letters.
- Address envelopes and fold letters.

LETTER OF APPLICATION

A letter of application is your introduction to an employer. It is a common way to ask for a job interview. Your letter will state what job you are applying for and why you are applying for it. You will write a letter of application

- when the employer you wish to contact lives in another city or town,
- as a cover letter when you are mailing a resume, or
- when you are answering a newspaper want ad or other job announcement.

Many people may apply for the same job, so your letter must create a good impression. It must attract attention, develop interest, and get action. Your letter will show how well you can communicate. Write all your letters so that they are interesting and accurate.

Guidelines for Writing Personal/Business Letters

In this unit, the block style letter format will be used. **Block style** is a format in which all letter parts begin at the left margin.

Letters can be written with two types of punctuation styles. **Mixed punctuation** requires a colon after the salutation and a comma after the complimentary close. The **salutation** is a greeting to the person receiving the letter. The

complimentary close is the ending in a letter. In **open punctuation,** no punctuation is used after the salutation or the complimentary close.

To write letters that create a good impression, follow these guidelines:

1. Key each letter neatly. Use correct grammar, spelling, and punctuation.
2. Include your address, the date, and your telephone number.
3. Address your letter to a specific person. Include name and title, company name, and address. If there is no name in a newspaper ad, you may call the business to get the name of the person you will write to.
4. Avoid starting the first sentence with the word *I.* Try not to overuse *I, me,* and *my* in your letter.
5. Limit your letter to one page.
6. In a letter of application, state the position you are applying for in the first paragraph. Close your letter by asking for an interview.
7. If you send a resume, use an enclosure notation.

Illustration 11-1 shows a person preparing to write a letter of application.

Illustration 11-1

Writing a Letter of Application

Parts of a Personal/Business Letter

There are five parts of a personal/business letter.

The return address and date are keyed about two inches from the top of the sheet. The **return address** is the writer's address and is keyed above the date.

The **letter address** includes the name and address of the person receiving the letter. The person's title and company name are included. Allow four to seven spaces between the date and letter address.

The **salutation** is a greeting to the person receiving the letter. Leave one blank space before and after the salutation.

The **body** is the message in a letter. Paragraphs are single spaced. Leave one blank space between paragraphs.

The **complimentary close** is the ending in a letter. Leave one blank space between the complimentary close and the last paragraph. Leave four blank spaces between the complimentary close and the writer's name. This space is for the writer's signature. The **signature** is the writer's name as written by that person. Be sure your signature is legible.

Illustration 11-2 shows the five parts of a business letter. Open punctuation is used in the letter.

CHECKPOINT 11-1

YOUR GOAL:
Get 5 or more answers correct.

Match the items in the left column with the definitions in the right column. Write the correct letter in each of the spaces provided. The first one is completed as as example.

_____e_____ ● Open punctuation

_____ 1. Salutation

_____ 2. Body

_____ 3. Mixed punctuation

_____ 4. Return address

_____ 5. Block style

_____ 6. Complimentary close

_____ 7. Letter address

a. Greeting

b. Writer's address

c. Name and address of person receiving letter

d. Ending of letter

e. No punctuation after salutation or close

f. Message of letter

g. A colon after salutation and comma after close

h. All letter parts begin at the left margin

☞ *Check your work. Record your score.*

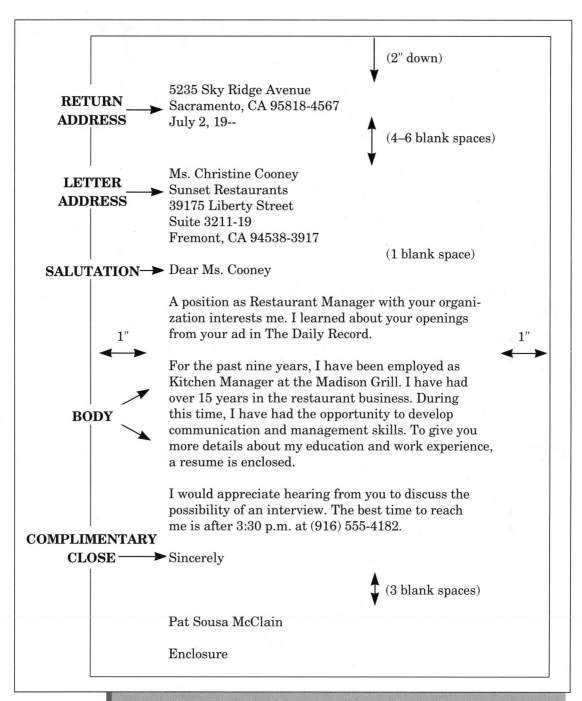

Illustration 11-2

Personal/Business Letter with Open Punctuation

GETTING READY TO GO TO WORK—Tips for Women Going to Interviews

- Wear clothes appropriate for the job.
- Wear stockings or panty hose.
- Do not wear sandals or fancy shoes.
- Avoid excessive jewelry.
- Use make-up moderately.
- Do not wear overpowering perfume.
- Keep hair neat and away from your face.
- Have clean and shaped fingernails at a moderate length.

CHECKPOINT 11-2

YOUR GOAL:
Get 7 or more
answers correct.

Read the following newspaper job ad. Write a letter of application for one of the jobs—supervisory trainee, cashier, or salesclerk. Write your letter on a blank sheet of paper. Use open punctuation. If you have access to a computer or typewriter, key your letter.

> **Supervisory Trainees,
> Cashiers, and Salesclerks**
>
> Office Products Emporium now
> has openings. Looking for ener-
> getic, responsible individuals
> who would like to grow with our
> team. Send resume or apply in
> person.
> Susan Ogata, Manager
> Office Products Emporium
> 4320 Newton Street
> Washington, DC 20010-2432

☞ *Check your work. Record your score.*

GETTING READY TO GO TO WORK—Tips for Men Going to Interviews

- Wear clothes appropriate for the job. If you wear a suit, wear a tie.
- Keep hair clean and neat.
- Trim beard and mustache.
- Do not wear overpowering cologne.
- Keep fingernails clean and trimmed.

INTERVIEW FOLLOW-UP LETTER

An interview follow-up letter should be sent to the employer after an interview. Your letter expresses your appreciation and thanks for the interview. A follow-up letter gives you one more chance to get the job. Sending a letter shows the employer that you have a sincere interest in the job.

Rules for Writing an Interview Follow-up Letter

Guidelines 1 through 5 for writing personal/business letters are used when writing an interview follow-up letter. In addition, your letter should include

1. a thank you for the interview, and
2. a statement to reaffirm your interest in the job and your availability.

Body of an Interview Follow-up Letter

The body of your follow-up letter will usually have three paragraphs.

The first paragraph will express your thanks for the interview. It will also state the position you applied for.

The second paragraph reaffirms your interest in the job. Say something about your education, work experience, and special skills.

The third and last paragraph will state your availability for the job. Illustration 11-3 is an example of an interview follow-up letter. The letter uses mixed punctuation.

✔ CHECKPOINT 11-3

YOUR GOAL:
Get 4 or more answers correct.

Each of the following statements about an interview follow-up letter is either true or false. Write *True* in the space provided next to each true statement. Write *False* in the space provided next to each false statement. The first one is completed as an example.

**True**   ● The follow-up letter has a salutation and complimentary close.

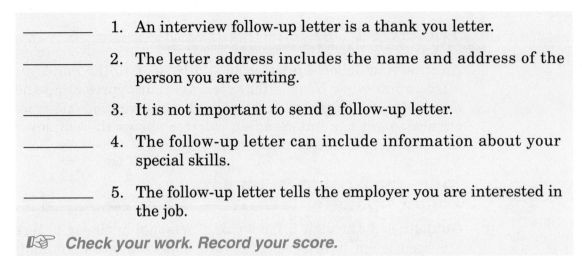

_____ 1. An interview follow-up letter is a thank you letter.

_____ 2. The letter address includes the name and address of the person you are writing.

_____ 3. It is not important to send a follow-up letter.

_____ 4. The follow-up letter can include information about your special skills.

_____ 5. The follow-up letter tells the employer you are interested in the job.

☞ *Check your work. Record your score.*

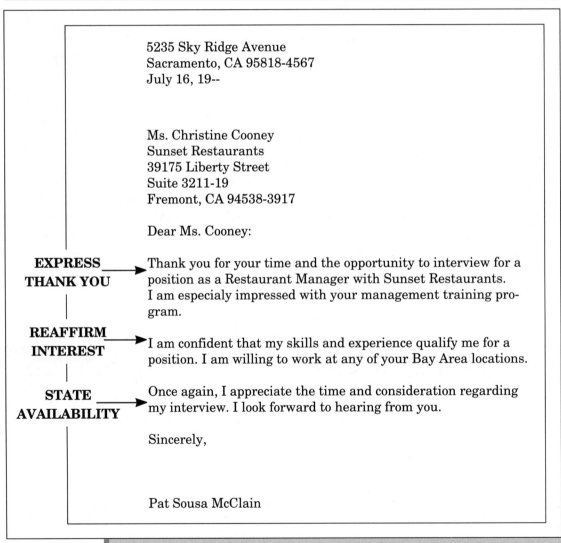

5235 Sky Ridge Avenue
Sacramento, CA 95818-4567
July 16, 19--

Ms. Christine Cooney
Sunset Restaurants
39175 Liberty Street
Suite 3211-19
Fremont, CA 94538-3917

Dear Ms. Cooney:

EXPRESS THANK YOU → Thank you for your time and the opportunity to interview for a position as a Restaurant Manager with Sunset Restaurants. I am especialy impressed with your management training program.

REAFFIRM INTEREST → I am confident that my skills and experience qualify me for a position. I am willing to work at any of your Bay Area locations.

STATE AVAILABILITY → Once again, I appreciate the time and consideration regarding my interview. I look forward to hearing from you.

Sincerely,

Pat Sousa McClain

Illustration 11-3

Interview Follow-up Letter with Mixed Punctuation

CHECKPOINT 11-4

YOUR GOAL:
Get 7 or more answers correct.

Write an interview follow-up letter. Your interview was last Tuesday with Ms. Susan Ogata, Manager. Write your letter on a blank sheet of paper. Use mixed punctuation. If you have access to a computer or typewriter, key your letter.

☞ *Check your work. Record your score.*

ADDRESSING ENVELOPES AND FOLDING LETTERS

After writing a letter, the next step is to prepare an envelope for the letter. The letter will then be folded and inserted into the envelope.

Addressing a Large Envelope

An envelope includes the return address of the writer. It also includes the name and address of the person who will receive the letter. Both addresses on the envelope should contain the two-letter state abbreviation and the ZIP Code. The state abbreviations will be covered in more detail in Unit 14.

The return address appears in the upper left corner of the envelope. The letter address begins on line 12 about 1/2 inch left of center. Both addresses are in all capital letters with no punctuation. Illustration 11-4 shows an example of the address format for a large envelope.

Illustration 11-4

Addressing Large Envelopes

Folding a Personal/Business Letter ━━━━━━

The correct procedure for folding a letter varies according to the size of the envelope. Illustration 11-5 shows the three steps for folding a letter into a large envelope.

Illustration 11-5

Folding Letters

Large Envelopes (Nos. 10, 9)

Step 1
With letter face up, fold slightly less than ⅓ of sheet up toward top.

Step 2
Fold down top of sheet to within ½ inch of bottom fold.

Step 3
Insert letter into envelope with last crease toward bottom of envelope.

✔ CHECKPOINT 11-5

YOUR GOAL:
Get 3 or more answers correct.

Key an envelope for the letter you wrote to Ms. Susan Ogata in Checkpoint 11-4. Fold the letter.

☞ *Check your work. Record your score.*

WHAT YOU HAVE LEARNED

As a result of completing this unit, you have learned that:
- Specific guidelines should be followed when writing personal/ business letters.
- There are five parts of a personal/business letter.
- After an interview, a follow-up letter should be sent.
- Addresses on envelopes are in capital letters.
- There is a correct way to fold a letter.

ACTIVITY 11-1 **YOUR GOAL:** Get 7 or more answers correct.

Pick a job from the Help Wanted section of your local newspaper for which you would like to apply. Write a letter of application on a blank sheet of paper. Use open punctuation.

☞ *Check your work. Record your score.*

ACTIVITY 11-2 **YOUR GOAL:** Get 3 or more answers correct.

Key an envelope for the letter you prepared in Activity 11-1. Fold and insert the letter.

☞ *Check your work. Record your score.*

PART FOUR
WRITING ON THE JOB

UNIT 12
FORMS

UNIT 13
MEMOS

UNIT 14
BUSINESS LETTERS

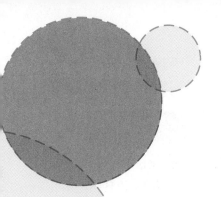

UNIT 12
FORMS

WHAT YOU WILL LEARN

When you finish this unit, you will be able to:
- Complete employment forms.
- Complete business sales slips.

EMPLOYMENT FORMS

In Unit 11, you learned about job application forms. There are three other forms to complete when you are hired for a job. One form asks for equal opportunity information. The other two forms are required by law: Form W-4, the Employee's Withholding Allowance Certificate, and Form I-9, the Employment Eligibility Verification.

Follow these basic rules when completing the forms:

1. Read the form carefully before starting to write.
2. Write neatly. Use a pen or key the information.
3. Be sure the information is accurate.
4. Sign your name legibly if your signature is required.

Equal Opportunity Information Form

All employers are required to provide an equal opportunity for employment to all persons. **Equal opportunity** means an employer will hire a person regardless of gender, sexual preference, race, creed, color, national origin, religion, handicap, or veteran's status. Employers keep track of this hiring practice. To do this, each applicant for a job is asked to complete a form. The form is completed on a voluntary basis. These forms vary with each company.

CHECKPOINT 12-1

YOUR GOAL:
Get 4 answers correct.

Review the completed Equal Opportunity Information Form on the left. Complete the blank form on the right with information about yourself.

Equal Opportunity Information Form

SEX
[X] M
[ ] F

ETHNICITY
[ ] African American
[ ] Asian
[ ] Spanish Surname
[ ] White
[ ] Pacific Islander
[X] American Indian
[ ] Filipino
[ ] Mexican American
[ ] Other (please specify)
_____

DISABILITY
[ ] None
[ ] Sight impaired
[X] Hearing impaired
[ ] Speech impaired
[ ] Upper limbs impaired
[ ] Lower limbs impaired
[ ] Other (please specify)
_____

VETERAN
[X] No
[ ] Vietnam-era
[ ] Other Veteran
[ ] Disabled Veteran

Equal Opportunity Information Form

SEX
[ ] M
[ ] F

ETHNICITY
[ ] African American
[ ] Asian
[ ] Spanish Surname
[ ] White
[ ] Pacific Islander
[ ] American Indian
[ ] Filipino
[ ] Mexican American
[ ] Other (please specify)
_____

DISABILITY
[ ] None
[ ] Sight impaired
[ ] Hearing impaired
[ ] Speech impaired
[ ] Upper limbs impaired
[ ] Lower limbs impaired
[ ] Other (please specify)
_____

VETERAN
[ ] No
[ ] Vietnam-era
[ ] Other Veteran
[ ] Disabled Veteran

☞ **Check your work. Record your score.**

Form W-4

Form W-4, Employee's Withholding Allowance Certificate, is a form completed for income tax withholding purposes. It is required by the Internal Revenue Service (IRS). Form W-4 tells your employer how much federal income tax should be withheld from your paycheck. Also on this form, you will declare your total number of allowances. An **allowance** is a person who is dependent on you for support. The more allowances you have, the less tax you will have withheld. Money withheld from your paycheck for federal income tax is paid directly to the Internal Revenue Service. State and city taxes may also be withheld from your paycheck.

A Personal Allowances Worksheet is part of Form W-4. It should be completed before filling in the W-4 section. You will give the employer only Form W-4—the certificate section.

You may claim yourself as an allowance. Other allowances can be claimed for your spouse or children. The following terms are included on the worksheet and Form W-4:

Dependents. People other than your wife or husband that you support. Children and elderly parents may be dependents.

Exempt Status. A claim that allows you to have no federal income tax withheld from your paycheck. You may claim to be exempt if you will not earn enough to owe any federal tax.

Head of Household. An unmarried person who pays more than 50 percent of household expenses.

Spouse. A wife or husband.

✔ **CHECKPOINT 12-2**

YOUR GOAL:
Get 10 or more answers correct.

Review the completed Personal Allowances Worksheet and Form W-4, Employee's Withholding Allowance Certificate. Complete the blank form that follows with information about yourself.

A	Enter "1" for **yourself** if no one else can claim you as a dependent	**A** _____
B	Enter "1" if: { **1.** You are single and have only one job; or **2.** You are married, have only one job, and your spouse does not work; or **3.** Your wages from a second job or your spouse's wages (or the total of both) are $1,000 or less. }	**B** _____
C	Enter "1" for your **spouse**. But, you may choose to enter "0" if you are married and have either a working spouse or more than one job (this may help you avoid having too little tax withheld)	**C** _____
D	Enter number of **dependents** (other than your spouse or yourself) whom you will claim on your tax return	**D** _____
E	Enter "1" if you will file as **head of household** on your tax return (see conditions under "Head of Household," above) . .	**E** _____
F	Enter "1" if you have at least $1,500 of **child or dependent care expenses** for which you plan to claim a credit	**F** _____
G	Add lines A through F and enter total here . . . . ▶	**G** _____

For accuracy, do all worksheets that apply.
- If you plan to **itemize or claim adjustments to income** and want to reduce your withholding, see the Deductions and Adjustments Worksheet on page 2.
- If you are **single** and have **more than one job** and your combined earnings from all jobs exceed $27,000 OR if you are **married** and have a **working spouse or more than one job**, and the combined earnings from all jobs exceed $46,000, see the Two-Earner/Two-Job Worksheet on page 2 if you want to avoid having too little tax withheld.
- If **neither** of the above situations applies, **stop here** and enter the number from line G on line 4 of Form W-4 below.

- **Cut here and give the certificate to your employer. Keep the top portion for your records.** -

Form **W-4** Department of the Treasury Internal Revenue Service	**Employee's Withholding Allowance Certificate** ▶ **For Privacy Act and Paperwork Reduction Act Notice, see reverse.**	OMB No. 1545-0010

1 Type or print your first name and middle initial	Last name	**2** Your social security number

Home address (number and street or rural route)	**3** Marital status	☐ Single ☐ Married ☐ Married, but withhold at higher Single rate.
City or town, state, and ZIP code		Note: *If married, but legally separated, or spouse is a nonresident alien, check the Single box.*

4 Total number of allowances you are claiming (from line G above or from the Worksheets on back if they apply) . . . | **4** |

5 Additional amount, if any, you want deducted from each pay . . . . | **5** $

6 I claim exemption from withholding and I certify that I meet **ALL** of the following conditions for exemption:
- Last year I had a right to a refund of **ALL** Federal income tax withheld because I had **NO** tax liability; **AND**
- This year I expect a refund of **ALL** Federal income tax withheld because I expect to have **NO** tax liability; **AND**
- This year if my income exceeds $550 and includes nonwage income, another person cannot claim me as a dependent.

If you meet all of the above conditions, enter the year effective and "EXEMPT" here . . . . . ▶ | **6** 19

7 Are you a full-time student? (**Note:** *Full-time students are not automatically exempt.*) . . . . | **7** ☐ Yes ☐ No

Under penalties of perjury, I certify that I am entitled to the number of withholding allowances claimed on this certificate or entitled to claim exempt status.

Employee's signature ▶   Date ▶   , 19

8 Employer's name and address (**Employer:** Complete 8 and 10 **only if sending to IRS**)	**9** Office code (optional)	**10** Employer identification number

A   Enter "1" for **yourself** if no one else can claim you as a dependent . . . . **A** _____

B   Enter "1" if: { 1. You are single and have only one job; or
                    2. You are married, have only one job, and your spouse does not work; or } . . **B** _____
                    3. Your wages from a second job or your spouse's wages (or the total of both) are $1,000 or less.

C   Enter "1" for your **spouse.** But, you may choose to enter "0" if you are married and have either a working spouse or
    more than one job (this may help you avoid having too little tax withheld) . . . . **C** _____

D   Enter number of **dependents** (other than your spouse or yourself) whom you will claim on your tax return . . . . . . **D** _____

E   Enter "1" if you will file as **head of household** on your tax return (see conditions under "Head of Household," above) . . **E** _____

F   Enter "1" if you have at least $1,500 of **child or dependent care expenses** for which you plan to claim a credit . . . . **F** _____

G   Add lines A through F and enter total here . . . . ▶ **G** _____

For accuracy,
do all
worksheets
that apply.
{ • If you plan to **itemize or claim adjustments to income** and want to reduce your withholding, see the Deductions and Adjustments Worksheet on page 2.
• If you are **single** and have **more than one job** and your combined earnings from all jobs exceed $27,000 OR if you are **married** and have a **working spouse or more than one job,** and the combined earnings from all jobs exceed $46,000, see the Two-Earner/Two-Job Worksheet on page 2 if you want to avoid having too little tax withheld.
• If **neither** of the above situations applies, **stop here** and enter the number from line G on line 4 of Form W-4 below. }

------------------------- **Cut here and give the certificate to your employer. Keep the top portion for your records.** -------------------------

Form **W-4**
Department of the Treasury
Internal Revenue Service

Employee's Withholding Allowance Certificate

▶ **For Privacy Act and Paperwork Reduction Act Notice, see reverse.**

OMB No. 1545-0010

1 Type or print your first name and middle initial   Last name   **2** Your social security number

Home address (number and street or rural route)

City or town, state, and ZIP code

3 Marital status
☐ Single ☐ Married
☐ Married, but withhold at higher Single rate.
Note: *If married, but legally separated, or spouse is a nonresident alien, check the Single box.*

4 Total number of allowances you are claiming (from line G above or from the Worksheets on back if they apply) . . . **4**

5 Additional amount, if any, you want deducted from each pay . . . . **5** $

6 I claim exemption from withholding and I certify that I meet **ALL** of the following conditions for exemption:
• Last year I had a right to a refund of **ALL** Federal income tax withheld because I had **NO** tax liability; **AND**
• This year I expect a refund of **ALL** Federal income tax withheld because I expect to have **NO** tax liability; **AND**
• This year if my income exceeds $550 and includes nonwage income, another person cannot claim me as a dependent.

If you meet all of the above conditions, enter the year effective and "EXEMPT" here . . . . . ▶ **6** | 19

7 Are you a full-time student? (**Note:** *Full-time students are not automatically exempt.*) . . . . **7** ☐ Yes ☐ No

Under penalties of perjury, I certify that I am entitled to the number of withholding allowances claimed on this certificate or entitled to claim exempt status.

Employee's signature ▶   Date ▶   , 19

8 Employer's name and address (**Employer:** Complete 8 and 10 **only if sending to IRS**)   **9** Office code (optional)   **10** Employer identification number

☞ *Check your work. Record your score.*

◀ EVOLUTION OF WRITING—Writing Instruments

In the very early days, people used chalky rocks to make marks and pictures on cliffs and on the walls of caves. As writing and drawing became more precise, the Egyptians invented "pens" made of bamboo reeds. The quill pen, made of goose feathers, replaced the reed pen. These pens could be found everywhere except in the Orient where the Chinese used brushes made from animal hairs. Around 1400 A.D., Europeans discovered that graphite could be used to mark on various materials. This discovery lead to the invention of the lead pencil.

Form I-9

Any person hired for a job after November 6, 1986, must complete **Form I-9, Employment Eligibility Verification**. The Immigration and Naturalization Service requires this form. Form I-9 is a standard form used to verify that an individual is eligible to work in the United States.

The form asks for the employee's name, address, date of birth, birth name, and Social Security number. There is also a section that asks about the employee's immigration status. The term penalty of perjury appears on the form. Penalty of perjury means a person may be fined or go to prison for giving false information. The penalty of perjury also refers to your claim of being a citizen or alien who is authorized to work in the United States.

In addition to providing personal information on the I-9 Form, a person hired for a job is required to provide one or more documents that establish identity and employment eligibility. The documents an employer will need to examine are shown in Illustration 12-1.

One from List A

1. United States passport
2. Certificate of U.S. citizenship
3. Certificate of naturalization
4. Unexpired foreign passport with employment authorization

——————————————— OR ———————————————

One from List B	and	**One from List C**
1. State driver's license or I.D. with photograph		1. Original Social Security card
2. U.S. military identification card		2. Birth certificate
		3. Unexpired INS Employment Authorization

Illustration 12-1

Documents Required for Employment Verification

CHECKPOINT 12-3

YOUR GOAL:
Get 8 or more answers correct.

Review the completed Employment Eligibility Verification (Form I-9). Complete the blank form that follows with information about yourself.

EMPLOYMENT ELIGIBILITY VERIFICATION (Form I-9)

1 **EMPLOYEE INFORMATION AND VERIFICATION:** (To be completed and signed by employee.)

Name: (Print or Type) Last *Kimura,*	First *Adam*	Middle *S.*	Birth Name *Kimura*
Address: Street Name and Number *324 Jackson*	City *Austin*	State *Texas*	ZIP Code *78731-1324*
Date of Birth (Month/Day/Year) *March 22, 1953*		Social Security Number *651-37-9436*	

I attest, under penalty of perjury, that I am (check a box):

☒ 1. A citizen or national of the United States.
☐ 2. An alien lawfully admitted for permanent residence (Alien Number A _____).
☐ 3. An alien authorized by the Immigration and Naturalization Service to work in the United States (Alien Number A _____ .
or Admission Number _____ , expiration of employment authorization, if any _____).

I attest, under penalty of perjury, the documents that I have presented as evidence of identity and employment eligibility are genuine and relate to me. I am aware that federal law provides for imprisonment and/or fine for any false statements or use of false documents in connection with this certificate.

Signature *Adam S. Kimura*	Date (Month/Day/Year) *June 5, 19--*

EMPLOYMENT ELIGIBILITY VERIFICATION (Form I-9)

1 **EMPLOYEE INFORMATION AND VERIFICATION:** (To be completed and signed by employee.)

Name: (Print or Type) Last	First	Middle	Birth Name
Address: Street Name and Number	City	State	ZIP Code
Date of Birth (Month/Day/Year)		Social Security Number	

I attest, under penalty of perjury, that I am (check a box):

☐ 1. A citizen or national of the United States.
☐ 2. An alien lawfully admitted for permanent residence (Alien Number A _____).
☐ 3. An alien authorized by the Immigration and Naturalization Service to work in the United States (Alien Number A _____ ,
or Admission Number _____ , expiration of employment authorization, if any _____).

I attest, under penalty of perjury, the documents that I have presented as evidence of identity and employment eligibility are genuine and relate to me. I am aware that federal law provides for imprisonment and/or fine for any false statements or use of false documents in connection with this certificate.

Signature	Date (Month/Day/Year)

☞ **Check your work. Record your score.**

BUSINESS SALES SLIPS

One of the most common business forms is a sales slip. This form is a record for the customer and the business. A sales slip shows what was purchased and how much was paid. Some sales slips are designed for specific businesses. Others are general. They can be used for many types of businesses.

A sales slip designed for a beauty salon is shown in Illustration 12-2. The date, time, and customer name are written at the top of the form. All the services offered by the salon are listed. The services used by the customer are checked off. Because prices increase or change, the price must be written for each service. The hair stylist writes his or her name in the left column. Retail items such as shampoos, brushes, combs, and other products are written on the bottom.

Illustration 12-2

Sales Slip for a Specific Business

RIKI SALON

24 Sutter Lane
San Francisco, CA 94108-2102
(415) 555-4466

DATE _11/3_   TIME _1 p.m._

NAME _M. Carter_

STYLIST	SERVICE		PRICE	
Brandi	FEM HAIR CUT	✓	12	00
	MALE HAIR CUT			
	COLOUR			
	TINT			
	PERM			
	PART PERM WAVE			
	RELAXER			
	SHAMPOO/BLOW DRY			
	FACIAL			
	MANICURE/PEDICURE			
	MAKE-UP/LESSON			
	MISC			

RETAIL TICKET

STOCK	PRICE
Shampoo	2.50
TOTAL	

AMOUNT DUE		
SERVICE	12	00
RETAIL	2	50
TAX		18
TOTAL $	14	68

Services are not taxed. Sales tax is figured on the retail items only. Sales tax varies in each city and state. The total for services are added to the retail items plus tax. A final total is written last. Addition should be checked.

A general sales slip that could be used by many businesses is shown in Illustration 12-3. The date and customer's name and address are written at the top. The salesperson's name is written at the bottom. A cash or charge sale is checked. A charge sale usually means the customer is using a credit card to purchase the merchandise or service. If the purchase is to be mailed to another location, that information is included.

Illustration 12-3

General Use
Sales Slip

SPORTS UNLIMITED
458 PARK ST.
BOSTON, MA 02107-1234
(617) 555-3846

DATE 4/23   19

SOLD TO *Pete Barnes*

ADDRESS *42 Country Dr., Reno, NV 89501-3412*

SHIP TO

ADDRESS

QUANTITY	DESCRIPTION	PRICE	AMOUNT	
1	*Nylon Jacket*		39	99
1	*Sunglasses*		5	00
		TAX	2	70
		TOTAL	47	69

CASH ✓   CHARGE   SOLD BY *Pam*

Each purchase must be written in the space provided. Quantity, description, price of each item, and totals are written. Tax is calculated to find the amount of the total sale.

CHECKPOINT 12-4

YOUR GOAL: Get 10 answers correct.

Complete the sales slip. Include the following:

Date: Current date

Sold To: Barry Cowan

Address: 1248 Oak St.

Denver, CO

80232-1248

Sold By: KYT

How Purchased: Charge

Quantity: One pair

Description: J.V. Sports Shoes

Price: $29.95

Tax: $1.80

Total: $31.75

SPORTS UNLIMITED
458 PARK ST.
BOSTON, MA 02107-1234
(617) 555-3846

DATE _____ 19 ___

SOLD TO

ADDRESS

SHIP TO

ADDRESS

QUANTITY	DESCRIPTION	PRICE	AMOUNT
		TAX	
		TOTAL	

CASH	CHARGE	SOLD BY

👉 *Check your work. Record your score.*

WHAT YOU HAVE LEARNED

As a result of completing this unit, you have learned:
- What information is asked on an equal opportunity form.
- What Form W-4 is, and how to complete the form.
- How to complete an I-9 Employment Eligibility Verification form.
- How to complete two different types of sales slips.

ACTIVITY 12-1   **YOUR GOAL:** Get 4 or more answers correct.

Answer the following questions about the completed Form W-4 in the space provided.

Form **W-4**	Employee's Withholding Allowance Certificate	OMB No. 1545-0010
Department of the Treasury Internal Revenue Service	▶ For Privacy Act and Paperwork Reduction Act Notice, see reverse.	

1 Type or print your first name and middle initial: Leo	Last name: Dameron	**2** Your social security number: 546-27-6831

Home address (number and street or rural route)
1746 E. Date Avenue

City or town, state, and ZIP code
Tampa, Florida   33624-1746

3 Marital status
☒ Single   ☐ Married
☐ Married, but withhold at higher Single rate.
Note: *If married, but legally separated, or spouse is a nonresident alien, check the Single box.*

4 Total number of allowances you are claiming (from line G above or from the Worksheets on back if they apply) . . . . **4** | 1

5 Additional amount, if any, you want deducted from each pay . . . . **5** $

6 I claim exemption from withholding and I certify that I meet **ALL** of the following conditions for exemption:
- Last year I had a right to a refund of **ALL** Federal income tax withheld because I had **NO** tax liability; **AND**
- This year I expect a refund of **ALL** Federal income tax withheld because I expect to have **NO** tax liability; **AND**
- This year if my income exceeds $550 and includes nonwage income, another person cannot claim me as a dependent.

If you meet all of the above conditions, enter the year effective and "EXEMPT" here . . . . . ▶ **6** | 19

7 Are you a full-time student? (**Note:** *Full-time students are not automatically exempt.*) . . . . **7** ☐ Yes ☐ No

Under penalties of perjury, I certify that I am entitled to the number of withholding allowances claimed on this certificate or entitled to claim exempt status.

Employee's signature ▶ *Leo Dameron*   Date ▶ 7/12 , 19 - -

8 Employer's name and address (**Employer:** Complete 8 and 10 **only if sending to IRS**) | **9** Office code (optional) | **10** Employer identification number

---

1. What is the employee's last name? _____

2. What is his Social Security number? _____

3. What is his marital status? _____

4. What city and state does he live in? _____

5. What is the total number of allowances he is claiming? _____

☞ *Check your work. Record your score.*

ACTIVITY 12-2 YOUR GOAL: Get 4 or more answers correct.

Answer the following questions about the completed sales in the space provided.

```
              SPORTS UNLIMITED
                  458 PARK ST.
             BOSTON, MA  02107-1234
                 (617) 555-3846

                        DATE 12/15    19--
  SOLD TO  Rachel Acosta
  ADDRESS  P.O. Box 523, Tucson, AZ 85713-0523
  SHIP TO
  ADDRESS
```

QUANTITY	DESCRIPTION	PRICE	AMOUNT
1	Shirt	15	15 00
2 pr.	Socks	4	8 00
1	Sports Cap	7	7 00
		TAX	1 80
		TOTAL	31 80

CASH ✓   CHARGE   SOLD BY Bob

1. What is the date of the sale? _____
2. What is the customer's name? _____
3. Was this a cash or charge sale? _____
4. How many items were purchased? _____
5. How much was the tax on the sale? _____

☞ *Check your work. Record your score.*

UNIT 13
MEMOS

WHAT YOU WILL LEARN

When you finish this unit, you will be able to:
- Write business memos.
- Use clear and concise writing.
- Identify non-biased writing.

BUSINESS MEMOS

A **memo** is a written communication used within an office or business. A memo is also called a *memorandum*. Memos are not as formal as letters. They may be written to communicate with just one person, or the same memo may be sent to several people. A memo may also be posted on a bulletin board for all employees to read.

Many businesses use standard memo stationery. Memos can also be on plain paper. Memos are keyed. A memo has a heading that includes these basic parts: TO, FROM, DATE, and SUBJECT. The *subject* line next to the subject head may or may not be capitalized. There are usually at least two blank lines between the heading and the first paragraph. A memo using company memo stationery is shown in Illustration 13-1.

The person sending the memo may initial the memo. The letters at the end of the memo are called *reference initials*. **Reference initials** tell who keyed the correspondence if it was not the sender. They are the first letters of the first and last names of that person.

COMPUTER
MARKETPLACE

Interoffice Memo

TO:	All Employees
FROM:	Arlene Lu, Personnel Director Ext. 4867
DATE:	October 15, 19—
SUBJECT:	HEALTH INSURANCE PROGRAM

A representative from the Stay-Well Health Plan will be here on November 10, 19—. The representative will talk about their new health plan. He will go over the cost of the rates for coverage.

The meeting is scheduled between 4:00–5:00 p.m., in Conference Room B. Please call me by November 8, if you will be attending. My number is Extension 4867.

jp

Illustration 13-1

Business Memo on Company Stationery

CLEAR AND CONCISE WRITING

Use clear and concise language when writing business letters and memos. Write as if you were talking to the person. Ask yourself, What do I want the reader to know, or what am I asking for? Use simple language. Do not use stiff or stuffy words. Use only the words needed to say what you mean. Short sentences are usually more effective than long, involved sentences. The following examples show how unneccessary words can be eliminated:

Say This	Do Not Say
enclosed	enclosed please find
thank you	want to thank you
please	we would appreciate
because	due to the fact that
we think	we wish to advise

CHECKPOINT 13-1

YOUR GOAL:
Get 4 or more
answers correct.

Review the memo. Answer the following questions about the memo in the spaces provided.

M E M O    **Memorial Hospital and Medical Center**

TO: All Employees

FROM: Arnold Stein, Manager
              Facilities Department

DATE: March 3, 19—

SUBJECT: Parking Lot C Resurfacing

Parking Lot C will be resurfaced on Friday, March 8. Please use Parking Lots A or B. Street parking is also available.

We regret this inconvenience and appreciate your cooperation during the resurfacing.

ef

---

1. Who is the memo from? _____

2. What is the subject of the memo? _____

3. What date is Parking Lot C being resurfaced? _____

4. Where should employees park? _____

5. What are the reference initials? _____

☞ *Check your work. Record your score.*

 CHECKPOINT 13-2

YOUR GOAL:
Get 4 or more
answers correct.

Write a memo to your supervisor requesting two weeks' vacation. The two weeks are June 12–26. Your supervisor's name is Ms. Lilly Dong. Use the current date. If possible, key your memo. Use the memo stationery provided. Answer the following questions about your memo in the space provided.

Thompson
PRODUCTS

PARTS · TOOLS · ACCESSORIES

Inter-Office Memorandum

TO:

FROM:

DATE:

SUBJECT:

1. Who is the memo written to? _____

2. What is the subject of the memo? _____

3. Did you key reference initials? _____

4. Who is the memo from? _____

5. Are the vacation dates included? _____

☞ *Check your work. Record your score.*

EVOLUTION OF WRITING—Early Typewriters

In 1868, Christopher Latham Sholes patented the typewriter. It only printed capital letters. Ten years later, the shift key was invented, and the typewriter could also print lowercase letters. In 1905, Sears sold a portable typewriter that was small enough to fit into a pocket. It cost $3.90.

NON-BIASED WRITING

In any type of business writing, titles and terms should be non-biased. Non-biased language does not favor female or male gender. Gender-neutral terms are used. The following are non-biased terms:

Say This	Do Not Say
work force	manpower
supervisor	foreman
firefighter	fireman
police officer	policeman
mail carrier	mailman
flight attendant	stewardess
humanity, everyone	mankind
sales representative, salesclerk, or salesperson	salesman

✔ CHECKPOINT 13-3

YOUR GOAL:
Get 9 or more answers correct.

Read each pair of terms in the following list. Write the best term to use in the space provided. The first one is completed as an example.

____sales representative____   ● salesman/sales representative

_____   1. mail carrier/mailman

_____   2. fireman/firefighter

_____   3. enclosed please find/enclosed

_____   4. manpower/work force

_____   5. want to thank you/thank you

_____   6. we wish to advise/we think

_____   7. due to the fact that/because

_____   8. humanity/mankind

_____   9. stewardess/flight attendant

_____   10. supervisor/foreman

☞ *Check your work. Record your score.*

WHAT YOU HAVE LEARNED

As a result of completing this unit, you have learned that:
- A memo is used within an office or business.
- Memos can be keyed on memo stationery or plain paper.
- Clear and concise language should be used.
- Non-biased language should be used.

ACTIVITY 13-1   YOUR GOAL: Get 4 or more answers correct.

Review the memo. Answer the following questions about the memo by writing *Yes* or *No* in the space provided. The first one is completed as an example.

> TO: All Employees
>
> FROM: Janet Russo, General Manager
>
> SUBJECT: HOLIDAY PARTY
>
> Plans for our annual Holiday Party are underway. This year's Holiday Party will be on December 16. It will be at the beautiful Palm Hotel.
>
> Albert Montoya, Salesman in the Appliance Department, is organizing the event. Please call him if you can serve on one of the committees. We need six people to work with him. We want your ideas to make this event a big success and an enjoyable evening.
>
> Please call Albert today!

_____Yes_____ ● Is the memo from Janet Russo, General Manager?

_____ 1. Does the heading include the date?

_____ 2. Should *Sales Representative* be used instead of *Salesman*?

_____ 3. Is a telephone number included for people to call?

_____ 4. Are reference initials included?

_____ 5. Are correct punctuation and capitalization used?

☞ *Check your work. Record your score.*

ACTIVITY 13-2   YOUR GOAL: Get 4 or more answers correct.

You are currently driving to work. There are several people from your company who live near you. You would like to start a car pool. You want to meet with anyone who is interested. Write a memo to your co-workers about your idea. Set a date, place, and time to meet. Use the memo stationery provided. Answer the questions about your memo that follow in the space provided.

Memo

$\mathcal{C}$arla's
$\mathcal{C}$abinet
$\mathcal{C}$onstruction

TO:

FROM:

DATE:

SUBJECT:

1. Who is the memo written to? _____

2. What is the subject of the memo? _____

3. Who is the memo from? _____

4. Does the memo include a date, time, and place to meet? _____

5. Are there at least two blank spaces between the subject and the first

    paragraph? _____

☞ *Check your work. Record your score.*

ACTIVITY 13-3 **YOUR GOAL:** Get 4 or more answers correct.

Rewrite the following sentences using non-biased terms.

1. Mankind would be better off if our air was not polluted.

    _____

2. She applied for a position as a mailman.

    _____

3. The fireman worked 24-hour shifts.

    _____

4. Ask the stewardess for a blanket.

    _____

5. The foreman praised his employees.

    _____

☞ *Check your work. Record your score.*

UNIT 14
BUSINESS LETTERS

WHAT YOU WILL LEARN

When you finish this unit, you will be able to:
- Write business letters.
- Use two-letter state abbreviations.
- Use the guidelines for writing business letters.
- Write business letters clearly and concisely.

BUSINESS LETTERS

A business letter is the most frequently used form of written communication in the business world. It is a formal way to send a message outside of the office or business. A letter has certain advantages over a telephone conversation. The following are some of the advantages of writing a business letter:

- The sender has time to organize what must be said.
- The receiver has a copy of the message that he or she can refer to as a reminder.
- A written message often has more impact than conversation.

Parts of a Business Letter

In Unit 11, you learned the five parts of personal letters. Those parts were return address, letter address, salutation, body, and complimentary close. A business letter has seven parts. In addition to the five parts covered in Unit 11, the business letter has these following parts: keyed signature and title and reference initials.

The **keyed signature and title** includes the name of the person sending the letter and his or her job title. The keyed signature and title follows the complimentary close. Four spaces are allowed in between for the handwritten signature.

The **reference initials** are the initials of the person who keyed the letter. Two or three initials can be used. They are usually lowercase letters. Reference initials were covered in Unit 13.

Some optional parts of a letter are notations for enclosures and copies. An **enclosure notation** is added when something is being sent with the letter. A **copy notation** indicates that a copy of the letter was sent to the person or persons named.

Modified Block Style Format

The style or format of a letter refers to the placement of the date, paragraphs, and close. The two most widely used styles are the *block style* and *modified block style* formats. Unit 11 contains information and sample letters in block style. You may want to refresh your memory by reviewing Unit 11.

All lines in the **modified block style** format begin at the left margin except for the dateline, complimentary close, and keyed signature and title. These parts begin at the center point. Illustration 14-1 shows a modified block style letter.

Addresses and Salutations in Business Letters

Personal and business letters include a letter address and a salutation. The salutation matches the letter address. If the letter address is to a person, the salutation includes the name. For example, the salutation in a letter to Mr. David Valdez would be *Dear Mr. Valdez*. If the letter address is to a company, the salutation is *Ladies and Gentlemen*. The letter address always includes number and street name, city, two-letter state abbreviation, and ZIP Code. Many addresses use the ZIP Code plus four digits.

Closings in Business Letters

The most commonly used closings are *Very truly yours* and *Sincerely*. Other acceptable closings are *Sincerely yours* and *Yours very truly*. Capitalize the first letter of the first word.

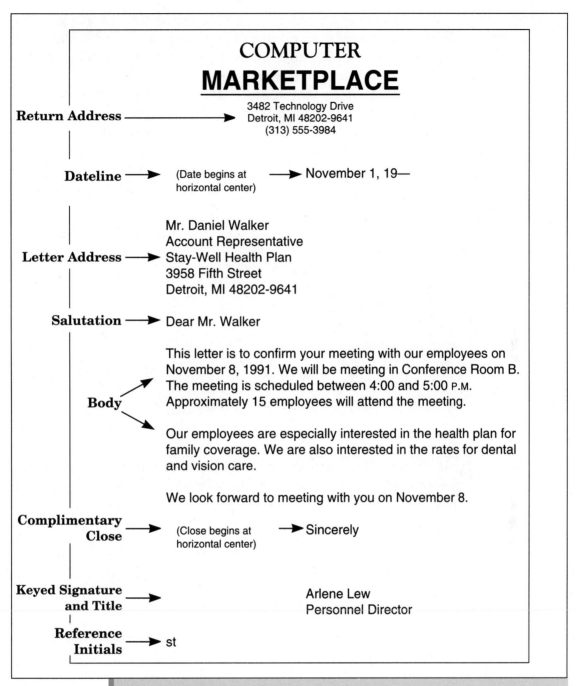

Return Address ————————→ COMPUTER **MARKETPLACE**
3482 Technology Drive
Detroit, MI 48202-9641
(313) 555-3984

Dateline ——→ (Date begins at ——→ November 1, 19—
horizontal center)

Mr. Daniel Walker
Account Representative
Letter Address ——→ Stay-Well Health Plan
3958 Fifth Street
Detroit, MI 48202-9641

Salutation ——→ Dear Mr. Walker

This letter is to confirm your meeting with our employees on
November 8, 1991. We will be meeting in Conference Room B.
Body The meeting is scheduled between 4:00 and 5:00 P.M.
Approximately 15 employees will attend the meeting.

Our employees are especially interested in the health plan for
family coverage. We are also interested in the rates for dental
and vision care.

We look forward to meeting with you on November 8.

Complimentary
Close ——→ (Close begins at ——→ Sincerely
horizontal center)

Keyed Signature
and Title ——→ Arlene Lew
Personnel Director

Reference
Initials ——→ st

Illustration 14-1

Modified Block Style Letter

EVOLUTION OF WRITING—The Postal Service

The U.S. Postal Service is the largest single business in the world. The first Postal Act was added to the U.S. Constitution in 1789. The cost of mailing a letter was based on distance. One-page letters were charged as follows: not over 30 miles, 6 cents; not over 80 miles, 10 cents; not over 100 miles, 12.5 cents; greater distances, 25 cents. The first stamps were printed in 1847. The 10-cent Washington stamp and the 5-cent Franklin stamp were the first stamps issued. Today, the U.S. Postal Service moves over a half-billion pieces of mail every day. The use of high-speed electronic scanning equipment makes this possible.

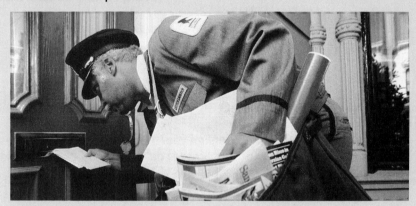

✔ CHECKPOINT 14-1

YOUR GOAL:
Get 9 or more answers correct.

Rewrite each of the following addresses in correct business letter format in the space provided. Write the correct salutation after each address. The first one is completed as an example.

● Dr. Marilyn Chen, Valley Medical Center, 297 Speedway, Tucson, AZ 85711-8712. Use mixed punctuation.

Dr. Marilyn Chen

Valley Medical Center

297 Speedway

Tucson, AZ 85711-8712

Dear Dr. Chen:

1. Mr. Isiah Walton, General Manager, Las Posas Auto Parts, 4987 Las Posas Street, Chicago, IL 60605-7243. Use open punctuation.

2. Mrs. Nan Ott, Personnel Department, American Electronics Corporation, 765 Moana Blvd., Suite 34, Honolulu, HI 96813-7374. Use mixed punctuation.

1. _____   2. _____

   _____   _____

   _____   _____

   _____   _____

   _____   _____

☞ *Check your work. Record your score.*

TWO-LETTER STATE ABBREVIATIONS

The United States Postal Service has devised a two-letter state abbreviation for each state name. This abbreviation is used with a postal ZIP Code on all addresses. The two-letter state abbreviations are shown in Illustration 14-2. Study this listing so that you know each state's two-letter abbreviation.

Alabama ....AL	Idaho ....ID	Missouri ....MO	Pennsylvania............PA
Alaska ....AK	Illinois........................IL	Montana ....MT	Rhode Island ....RI
Arizona ....AZ	Indiana ....IN	Nebraska............NE	South Carolina ....SC
Arkansas................AR	Iowa...........................IA	Nevada...............NV	South Dakota ....SD
California................CA	Kansas ....KS	New Hampshire ..NH	Tennesse ....TN
Colorado................CO	Kentucky ....KY	New Jersey..........NJ	Texas ....TX
Connecticut ....CT	Louisiana ....LA	New Mexico........NM	Utah ....UT
Delaware.................DE	Maine......................ME	New York ....NY	Vermont....................VT
District of	Maryland ....MD	North Carolina.....NC	Virginia ....VA
Columbia..............DC	Massachusetts ....MA	North Dakota.......ND	Washington ....WA
Florida.....................FL	Michigan ....MI	Ohio ....OH	West Virginia..........WV
Georgia...................GA	Minnesota................MN	Oklahoma ....OK	Wisconsin ....WI
Hawaii ....HI	Mississippi ....MS	Oregon...............OR	Wyoming ....WY

Illustration 14-2

Two-Letter State Abbreviations

✔ CHECKPOINT 14-2

YOUR GOAL:
Get 9 or more
answers correct.

Write the two-letter state abbreviation in the space provided next to each of the following state names. The first one is complete as an example.

___TX___ • Texas

_____ 1. Nebraska   _____ 2. West Virginia

_____ 3. Tennessee   _____ 4. South Dakota

_____ 5. New York   _____ 6. Oklahoma

_____ 7. Montana   _____ 8. Alaska

_____ 9. Iowa   _____ 10. Mississippi

☞ *Check your work. Record your score.*

GUIDELINES FOR WRITING LETTERS

These guidelines should be followed when writing a letter:

1. Plan your letters. Think about your purpose for writing before you begin.
2. Choose your words carefully. Be businesslike, but also be sincere and friendly. Use clear and concise language.
3. Be courteous. Show your readers that you respect them.
4. Be positive. Avoid negative words or accusations.
5. Be consistent in the format you use. If the date begins at the left margin, the closing should also begin at the left margin.
6. Letters should be keyed whenever possible. The dateline is keyed on line 16 for an average letter. Margins will be determined by the length of the letter.
7. Proofread letters for sentence structure, punctuation, capitalization, and spelling.

CLEAR AND CONCISE WRITING

Business letters are written to request something, to share information, or to follow-up on a request. Whatever the reason for writing, letters should be clear and concise. This will allow the reader to understand what the writer means and will avoid confusion.

The following are examples of the way to make letter writing clearer:

Example: Our copy machine is broken so we need to replace it. We are interested in buying one of your machines. Can your sales representative call us?

This is clearer:

Our office is interested in buying a new copy machine. We will be replacing our existing machine.

Please send us some information about your copy machines. We would also like a price list.

Please have your sales representative call us sometime next week.

Example: Sign and return the enclosed form as soon as possible.

This is clearer:

Please sign and return the enclosed form by January 15, 19—.

Example: You are invited to a retirement dinner for Martin Medina. It will be at the Oceanview Hotel on July 30. We hope you can attend.

This is clearer:

You are invited to a retirement dinner honoring Martin Medina. The dinner will be held at the Oceanview Hotel on July 30 at 6 P.M.

We know Martin will be pleased if you can attend this special evening. Please let us know by June 15 if you will be able to join us.

CHECKPOINT 14-3

YOUR GOAL:
Get 6 or more
answers correct.

Write a letter to Ms. Anne Rossi, Sales Representative, Hi-Tech Business Machines, 3459 Grand Avenue, Detroit, Michigan 48202-2739.

The purpose of the letter is to tell Ms. Rossi of your company's plans to purchase a new computer. The computer is the XRT Model 348. You would like a price on the machine. You would also like to see a demonstration of the machine. Ask if the demonstration can be scheduled before May 15.

The letter is from Jim McBride, Purchasing Agent. Use modified block style and open punctuation. Use the current date. Key your letter if possible. Use blank paper. Assume that you have letterhead stationery in keying the dateline. Follow the guidelines for writing business letters.

Answer the following questions after keying or writing your letter. Write each answer in the space provided. The first one is completed as an example.

● What date did you use? _____ Current date _____

1. Where did you begin the date? _____

2. How many lines are in the letter address? _____

3. What is the salutation? _____

4. What computer did you write about? _____

5. How many spaces are before and after the salutation? _____

6. Where did you begin keying the closing? _____

7. What is the last part on the letter? _____

☞ *Check your work. Record your score.*

WHAT YOU HAVE LEARNED

As a result of completing this unit, you have learned that:
● There are seven parts in a business letter.
● The date and closing begin at the center point in a modified block style letter.
● Every state has a two-letter state abbreviation.
● Business letters must be written clearly and concisely.

ACTIVITY 14-1   **YOUR GOAL:** Get 4 or more answers correct.

Read the following letter. Answer the questions about the letter by writing *Yes* or *No* in the space provided. The first one is completed as an example.

Carla's Cabinet Construction

323 Broadway
Santa Monica, CA 90405-6838
(213) 555-9692

Sept 25, 19—

Mr. Arnold Rosenberg
Maintenance Supervisor
Heavy-Duty Maintenance Company
491 Industrial Parkway
Los Angeles, CA 90025-7463

Dear Mr. Rosenberg:
We are very dissatisfied with the equipment maintenance service we have received from your company. It is very important that your representative service our equipment once a month, as is stated in our agreement with your company.

There have been only four service calls made to us in the past six months. As a result, we have twice had to call you to have a table saw repaired.

We have had a service agreement with you for over 10 years. We would appreciate your immediate attention to this problem.

Very truly yours,

Carla Jones-Reyes
Owner

tf

_____No_____ • Is the date written correctly?

_____ 1. Does the letter use block style?

_____ 2. Is the two-letter state abbreviation correct?

_____   3.   Is open punctuation used?

_____   4.   Should there be a double-space after the salutation?

_____   5.   Is the first paragraph written clearly?

_____   6.   Is there a double-space between each paragraph?

_____   7.   Should the closing begin at the left margin?

_____   8.   Is the closing capitalized correctly?

_____   9.   Are reference initials included?

_____   10.   Is the letter signed?

☞   *Check your work. Record your score.*

ACTIVITY 14-2   YOUR GOAL: Get 4 or more answers correct.

Write each letter in the space provided that correctly answers the following questions. The first one is completed as an example.

Which salutation uses mixed punctuation?

● ___*a*___   a.   Dear Dr. Oliver:

           b.   Dear Ms. Hughes

           c.   Dear Rev. Ogata

Which salutation uses mixed punctuation?

1. _____   a.   Dear Dr. Oliver

           b.   Dear Ms. Hughes:

           c.   Dear Rev. Ogata

Which closing uses open punctuation?

2. _____   a.   Sincerely yours,   3. _____   a.   Very truly yours,

           b.   Sincerely   b.   Sincerely yours,

           c.   Yours very truly,   c.   Sincerely,

Which two-letter state abbreviation is correct?

4. _____ a. Las Vegas, NE   5. _____ a. Seattle, WN

          b. Austin, TX   b. Maui, HA

          c. Anchorage, AL   c. Denver, CO

☞ *Check your work. Record your score.*

PART FIVE
WRITING FOR PERSONAL USE

YOUR SELF-IMPROVEMENT ACTION PLAN

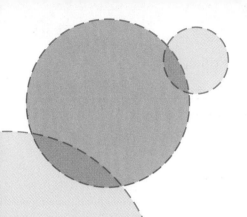

UNIT 15
YOUR SELF-IMPROVEMENT ACTION PLAN

WHAT YOU WILL LEARN

When you finish this unit, you will be able to:
- Understand why setting goals in twelve categories is important.
- Set short-term and long-term goals.
- Develop a self-improvement action plan.

SETTING GOALS

Goals give meaning to life. A **goal** is something you want to achieve. Setting goals is one way to direct your future. Some goals are short term. **Short-term goals** can be achieved in a few days, a week, a month, or a year. Other goals are long term. **Long-term goals** take two to five years or longer to reach. Meeting goals depends on your outlook, age, and the steps you take.

This unit will help you set personal goals. Based on these goals, you will develop a self-improvement action plan. This action plan will be completed by answering four questions about where you are and where you want to be. The four questions are shown in Illustration 15-1.

CATEGORIES FOR SETTING GOALS

Your life can be divided into twelve different categories. Some categories may be more important to you than others. Writing down goals in each category will help focus on what you want. These goals will guide you in writing your self-improvement action plan. You want to live a balanced life. You need goals in all categories to live a balanced life. In each category there are questions to answer. Those categories and some possible questions are as follows:

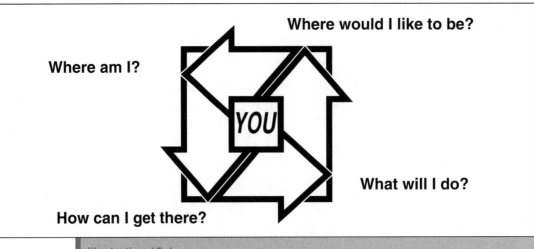

Illustration 15-1

Setting Goals—Four Questions to Answer

1. **Career.** If you are working, do you want a career change? If you are not working, what kind of job do you want? What will you look for in a job?

2. **Money.** How much money would you like to be earning? How much money do you spend? Would you like to save more?

3. **Education.** Would you like more job skills? Do you want to learn to play a musical instrument? Take a photography class or cooking class? Learn to use a computer?

4. **Social Relationships.** Would you like to have more friends? End some relationships? Improve some relationships?

5. **Family Relationships.** Would you like to improve communications with your spouse? Have a better understanding of your children? Be closer to relatives?

6. **Residence.** Would you like to move? Buy a house? Have another bedroom? Paint or redecorate?

7. **Transportation.** Would you like to buy a car? Would you like your present car to last longer?

8. **Travel.** Do you want to take a trip? Where would you go? For how long?

9. **Material Possessions.** What would you like to buy? A videocassette recorder? A new refrigerator? Is there something you would like to get rid of?

10. **Recreation.** What are your leisure-time activities? Do you make time for some fun in your life? Read a book once a month? Go to a movie or ball game?

11. **Physical Health.** Are you in good health? Would you like to exercise regularly? Lose five pounds? Get a physical checkup? Do you eat healthy foods?

12. **Wild Card.** This wild card category is a catch-all. What other areas do you want to work on? Do you have spiritual needs? Want to build your self-confidence?

This list will help you decide what you want from life. It will help you find out what is important to you. Answering these questions is the first step in writing your personal goals. There may be other questions you must answer for yourself. You need to be realistic when setting goals. Set goals that you can reach.

✔ CHECKPOINT 15-1

YOUR GOAL:
Complete 24 boxes.

Write down what you would like to be, do, or have in each category. Write one short-term goal and one long-term goal in each box. The Wild Card space is for you to create your own category. The first one is completed as an example.

Category	Short-Term Goals (Within one year)	Long-Term Goals (Two to five years)
● Career	*Complete high school computer accounting course.*	*Go to college to become an accountant.*
1. Career		
2. Money		

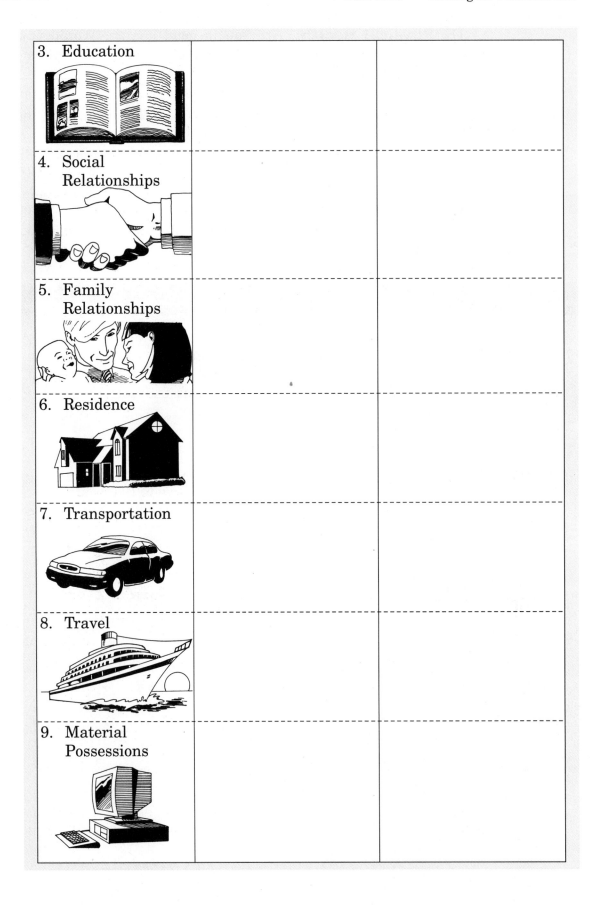

3. Education		
4. Social Relationships		
5. Family Relationships		
6. Residence		
7. Transportation		
8. Travel		
9. Material Possessions		

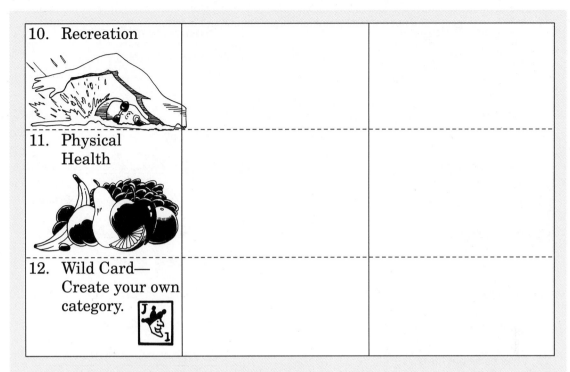

10. Recreation		
11. Physical Health		
12. Wild Card— Create your own category.		

☞ *Check your work. Record your score.*

DEVELOPING YOUR ACTION PLAN

Goals are achieved by taking action. A plan for the action assures achievement within a set amount of time. To develop your action plan for your short- and long-term goals, you will need to answer these four questions:

1. *Where am I?* What you are now doing.
2. *Where would I like to be?* Your short- or long-term goal.
3. *How can I get there?* What you need to do.
4. *What will I do?* The actual action steps you will take to meet your goals. Be specific.

An example of how to answer these four questions is shown in Illustration 15-2. The category Money and a short-term goal are used.

Category	Short-Term Goal
Money	Develop a Monthly Budget

ACTION PLAN

1. Where am I?

   I do not budget or manage money wisely.

2. Where would I like to be?

   Become a better money manager.

3. How can I get there?

   Live within my monthly budget.

4. What will I do?

   a.) Keep track of daily and weekly expenses.

   b.) Don't buy things I don't need.

   c.) Plan meals around sales items or use food coupons.

Illustration 15-2

Self-Improvement Action Plan

WRITING GEMS—Don't Quit

When things go wrong as they sometimes will,
When the road you're trudging seems all uphill,
When the funds are low, and the debts are high,
And you want to smile, but you have to sigh,
When care is pressing you down a bit—
Rest if you must, but
don't you quit.

Success is failure turned inside out,
The silver tint of the clouds of doubt.
And you never can tell how close you are,
It may be near when it seems afar.
So, stick to the fight when you're hardest hit—
It's when things go wrong that
you mustn't quit.

Anonymous

CHECKPOINT 15-2

YOUR GOAL:
Get 4 or more answers.

Pick the category from Checkpoint 15-1 that is most important to you. Develop your action plan using the short-term goal you wrote for that category. Answer all four questions. Write in the space provided.

Category	**Short-Term Goal**
_____	_____
	_____
	_____

ACTION PLAN

1. Where am I?

_____

_____

2. Where would I like to be?

_____

_____

3. How can I get there?

_____

_____

4. What will I do?

_____

_____

_____

_____

_____

_____

_____

☞ *Check your work. Record your score.*

WHAT YOU HAVE LEARNED

As a result of completing this unit, you have learned that:

● Setting short-term and long-term goals is one way to direct your future.
● Goals in all twelve categories are needed for living a balanced life.
● Four questions need to be answered to develop an action plan.

ACTIVITY 15-1   **YOUR GOAL:** Get 4 or more answers.

Pick another category from Checkpoint 15-1. Develop your action plan using the long-term goal you wrote in that category. Write in the spaces provided.

Category	**Long-Term Goal**
_____	_____
	_____
	_____

ACTION PLAN

1. Where am I?	4. What will I do?
_____	_____
_____	_____
	_____
2. Where would I like to be?	_____
_____	_____
_____	_____
3. How can I get there?	_____
_____	_____

☞ *Check your work. Record your score.*

APPENDIX A
Commonly Used Irregular Verbs

PRESENT	PAST	PRESENT	PAST
am	was	lead	led
awake	awoke, awaked	leave	left
bear	bore	lie (rest)	lay
become	became	lose	lost
begin	began	make	made
bend	bent	mean	meant
bite	bit	meet	met
blow	blew	pay	paid
break	broke	ride	rode
bring	brought	ring	rang
burn	burned, burnt	rise	rose
burst	burst	run	ran
catch	caught	say	said
choose	chose	see	saw
come	came	sell	sold
dig	dug	set	set
do	did	shake	shook
draw	drew	shrink	shrank
drink	drank	sing	sang
drive	drove	sink	sank
eat	ate	sit	sat
fall	fell	sleep	slept
fight	fought	slide	slid
find	found	speak	spoke
fly	flew	spend	spent
forget	forgot	spring	sprang
forgive	forgave	stand	stood
freeze	froze	steal	stole
get	got	sting	stung
give	gave	strike	struck
go	went	sweep	swept
grow	grew	swim	swam
hang	hung, hanged	swing	swung
have	had	tear	tore
hear	heard	tell	told
hide	hid	think	thought
keep	kept	throw	threw
know	knew	wear	wore
lay (to place)	laid	write	wrote

This is only a partial list of irregular verbs. Check grammar books for additional irregular verbs.

APPENDIX B
Frequently Used Prepositions

aboard	below	in	since
about	beneath	inside	through
above	beside	into	throughout
across	between	like	to
after	beyond	near	toward
against	by	of	under
along	down	off	underneath
among	during	on	until
around	except	out	unto
at	for	out of	up
as	from	outside	upon
because	from among	over	with
before	from between	past	within
behind	from under	round	without

Check the dictionary or grammar books for additional prepositions.

GLOSSARY

A

Adjective A word used to describe a noun or pronoun.

Adverb A word used to tell more about a verb, adjective, or another adverb.

Allowance A person who is dependent on you for support.

Antecedent The noun to which the pronoun refers.

Appositive A word or group of words that rename a noun.

B

Block Style A letter format in which all parts begin at the left margin.

Body Sentences that support the topic of the paragraph. Also the message in a letter.

C

Capitalization The use of capital letters.

Complimentary Close The ending in a letter.

Compound Sentence A sentence in which two or more ideas are combined into the same sentence.

Conjunction A word that connects individual words or groups of words.

Consonants All letters of the alphabet other than the vowels *a, e, i, o, u,* and sometimes *y.*

Contraction A shorter way of writing some pairs of words.

Copy Notation Indicates that a copy of the letter was sent to the person or persons named.

D

Dependents People other than your wife or husband that you support. Children and elderly parents may be dependents.

E

Enclosure Notation Indicates that something is being sent with the letter.

Ending or **Concluding Sentence** The last sentence in a paragraph. It comes after all details have been included in the body of the paragraph.

Equal Opportunity Hiring practice in which an employer will hire a person regardless of gender, sexual preference, race, creed, color, religion, handicap, or veteran's status.

Exempt Status A claim that allows you to have no federal income tax withheld from your paycheck. You may claim to be exempt if you will not earn enough to owe any federal tax.

F

Form I-9 Employment Eligibility Verification A standard form used to verify that an individual is eligible to work in the United States.

Form W-4, Employee's Withholding Allowance Certificate A form completed for income tax withholding purposes.

G

Gender Refers to feminine (she), masculine (he), or neuter (it).

Goal Something you want to achieve.

H

Head of Household An unmarried person who pays more than 50 percent of household expenses.

I

Independent Clause A group of words that has a subject and a verb.

Interjection A word or words used to express strong emotion or surprise.

K

Keyed Signature and Title The name of the person sending the letter and his or her job title.

L

Letter Address The name and address of the person receiving the letter.

Long-Term Goal A goal that can be achieved in two to five years or longer.

M

Memo A written communication used within an office or business.

Mixed Punctuation A colon after the salutation, and comma after the complimentary close.

Modified Block Style A letter format in which all lines in a letter begin at the left margin except for the dateline and complimentary close.

Modifier A word that tells more about another word.

N

Noun A word that names a person, place, thing, or idea.

Number Singular (one) or plural (more than one) in subject-verb agreement.

O

Open Punctuation No punctuation after the salutation or complimentary close.

P

Paragraph A group of sentences about one idea or subject.

Parts of Speech Refers to how words are used in sentences. The eight parts of speech are noun, pronoun, verb, adjective, adverb, preposition, conjunction, and interjection.

Penalty of Perjury A person may be fined or go to prison for giving false information.

Predicate A word that tells about the subject.

Preposition A word or group of words that shows how two words or ideas are related to each.

Pronoun A word used in place of a noun.

Punctuation Marks Symbols used to add clarity to writing.

R

Reference Initials The first letters of the first and last names of the person who keyed the correspondence if it was not the sender.

Resume A summary of a person's background and qualifications.

Return Address The writer's address.

Run-On Sentence Two or more sentences that run together because of incorrect or no punctuation.

S

Salutation A greeting to the person receiving the letter.

Sentence One or more words that give a complete idea.

Sentence Fragment A group of words that does not sound complete.

Short-Term Goal A goal that can be achieved in a few days, a week, a month, or a year.

Signature The name of the letter writer as written by that person.

Simple Sentence A sentence that has one independent clause.

Spouse A wife or husband.

Subject The part of a sentence that tells who or what is doing something. Or it tells who or what is being described.

T

Topic Sentence The first sentence in a paragraph. It tells what the paragraph is going to be about.

V

Verb A word that expresses an action.

Vowels The letters a, e, i, o, u, and sometimes y.

ACKNOWLEDGMENTS

Chapter 2   page 14, © Joel Gordon; page 15a, FPG International/Richard Laird; page 15b, FPG International/Lee Foster

Chapter 5   page 70, BMPorter/Don Franklin; page 71, © Freda Leinwand; page 72, © Woodfin Camp & Associates, Inc./Will Rhyins; page 73, FPG International/Bernice Johnson

Chapter 7   page 89a, 89b, © Joel Gordon

Chapter 8   page 103a, FPG International/Bernice Johnson; page 103b, BMPorter/Don Franklin

Chapter 11   page 135, © Paul Buddle

Chapter 13   page 161, © Bettman Archive

Chapter 14   page 170, FPG International/Tracey T

INDEX

ANSWERS

UNIT 1

CHECKPOINT 1-1, page 3

1. O. J. Simpson
2. The original painting
3. The child
4. Dr. Fung
5. The President

CHECKPOINT 1-2, page 4

1. O. J. Simpson
2. The original painting
3. The child
4. Dr. Fung
5. The President

CHECKPOINT 1-3, page 6

1. Lenora, Bill
2. Mei Ching
3. Computers, copiers
4. Walking
5. David Taylor

CHECKPOINT 1-4, page 6

1. exercise daily.
2. is common among adults.
3. was a civil rights leader.
4. are replacing records.
5. is a problem for the environment.

CHECKPOINT 1-5, page 7

1. exercise daily.
2. is common among adults.
3. was a civil rights leader.
4. are replacing records.
5. is a problem for the environment.

CHECKPOINT 1-6, page 9

1. plays
2. sang, danced
3. barked
4. moved
5. collect

CHECKPOINT 1-7, page 10

1. you
2. he
3. Hideo
4. you
5. apartment

ACTIVITY 1-1, page 11

1. <u>Virginia</u> and <u>John</u> <u>traveled</u> to <u>San Antonio</u> by <u>train.</u>
2. <u>Part-time jobs</u> <u>are</u> <u>available at the department store.</u>
3. <u>What</u> <u>is</u> your <u>favorite food?</u>
4. <u>Doug</u> and <u>Valerie</u> <u>saved</u> <u>to buy a home.</u>
5. <u>Karen</u> <u>dressed</u> <u>properly for the job interview.</u>
6. <u>Her parents</u> <u>were</u> <u>caring and encouraging.</u>
7. <u>The</u> <u>computer</u> <u>software</u> <u>requires a hard disk.</u>
8. <u>Pablo</u> <u>worked</u> <u>in</u> <u>advertising and construction.</u>
9. <u>The</u> <u>restaurant</u> <u>serves Cambodian food.</u>
10. <u>Mark</u> <u>attends junior high school.</u>

ACTIVITY 1-2, page 11

Words underlined once	Words underlined twice
1. Virginia, John	traveled
2. jobs	are
3. what	is
4. Doug, Valerie	saved
5. Karen	dressed
6. parents	were
7. software	requires
8. Pablo	worked
9. restaurant	serves
10. Mark	attends

ACTIVITY 1-3, page 12

plans
instructor
Miguel
receive
works
feeds
likes
plays
coaches
Consuelo

UNIT 2

CHECKPOINT 2-1, page 16

Person	**Place**
child	restaurant
manager	Grand Canyon
Ms. Guiterrez	office
drafter	Boston

Thing	**Idea**
food	joy
newspaper	love
September	stress
telephone	self-confidence

For the second part of Checkpoint 2-1, review your answers with two classmates. Give yourself 1 point for each correct noun.

CHECKPOINT 2-2, page 18

1. They
2. They
3. It
4. He
5. We

CHECKPOINT 2-3, page 19

1. trains
2. delivered
3. danced
4. yelled
5. is demonstrating

CHECKPOINT 2-4, page 21

1. lived	2. dragged
3. fried	4. praised
5. owed	6. hired

CHECKPOINT 2-5, page 22

1. ancient	2. deadly
3. positive	4. happy
5. generous	6. cold
7. patient	8. new
9. hardworking	10. skilled

CHECKPOINT 2-6, page 23

1. beautifully
2. slowly
3. carefully
4. legibly
5. tomorrow

CHECKPOINT 2-7, page 24

1. under
2. down
3. over
4. during
5. from

CHECKPOINT 2-8, page 25

1. and
2. yet
3. or
4. but
5. or

CHECKPOINT 2-9 page 26

1. Oh, no	2. Stop
3. Hooray	4. Ouch
5. Wonderful	

ACTIVITY 2-1, page 27

1. e	2. f
3. b	4. g
5. d	6. c
7. a	

ACTIVITY 2-2, page 27

1. George Washington Carver, peanut
2. highway, earthquake
3. holidays, weekends

4. it, they
5. you, I, you
6. she, it
7. are
8. worked, played
9. write, sing
10. summer
11. warm
12. yellow, cotton
13. weekly
14. quickly
15. loudly
16. to, on
17. with
18. beyond
19. or
20. and
21. but
22. Hooray
23. Step on it
24. Oh, no
25. Ouch

ACTIVITY 2-3, page 29

Review your sentences with a classmate.
Give yourself 1 point for each correct sentence.

UNIT 3

CHECKPOINT 3-1, page 32

Compare your uppercase and lowercase
letters with letters in Illustration 3-1.
Give yourself 1 point for each letter
written correctly.

CHECKPOINT 3-2, page 34

1. b.
   New Year's
   Lincoln Memorial, Washington, D.C.
2. a.
   Golden Gate Bridge, San Francisco
   Julianne, Saturday
3. b.
   Monday
   Detroit, Michigan

4. c.
   Lopez, Christmas Day
   We, Passover
5. c.
   What
   Mark Twain

CHECKPOINT 3-3, page 37

1. b.
   Department, Defense
   Red Cross
2. b.
   Volkswagen, Rabbit
   Compu-Shop
3. c.
   Duchess, York, United States
   Lyndon B. Johnson, Texas
4. c.
   Puerto Rican, Cuban, Korean
   First Baptist Church
5. b.
   Francisco
   Dad

CHECKPOINT 3-4, page 40

1. c.
   Ms. Kartes
   Reverend Okamoto
2. b.
   Sincerely
   Respectfully
3. c.
   EPCOT
   FDR
4. b.
   West
   South
5. a.
   I
   I

ACTIVITY 3-1, page 42

1. C., Penny, Christmas
2. Disneyland, Memorial Day
3. American Heart Association, Saturday
4. German, French, Spanish
5. Uncle Bob, Scottsdale Racquet Club

6. <u>R</u>ams, <u>V</u>ikings, <u>B</u>roncos
7. <u>M</u>artinez, <u>S</u>ave <u>M</u>oney <u>M</u>arket
8. <u>I</u>nternal <u>R</u>evenue <u>S</u>ervice
9. <u>A</u>frican-<u>A</u>merican, <u>R</u>ichmond, <u>V</u>irginia
10. <u>W</u>hile, <u>D</u>id
11. <u>D</u>ear, <u>M</u>s., <u>T</u>yson
12. <u>H</u>igh-<u>T</u>ech, <u>I</u>nc., <u>C</u>olorado
13. <u>S</u>herry, <u>E</u>ssex
14. <u>U</u>nited <u>N</u>ations, <u>N</u>ew <u>Y</u>ork
15. <u>C</u>harles, <u>K</u>ing, <u>E</u>ngland
16. <u>W</u>ould, <u>C</u>oca-<u>C</u>ola, <u>P</u>epsi
17. <u>T</u>im's, <u>F</u>irst <u>M</u>ethodist <u>C</u>hurch
18. <u>E</u>lizabeth, <u>M</u>ilwaukee <u>S</u>avings <u>L</u>oan
19. <u>E</u>ast <u>C</u>oast, <u>W</u>est <u>C</u>oast
20. <u>S</u>incerely
21. <u>T</u>hanksgiving <u>D</u>ay, <u>T</u>hursday
22. <u>I</u>, <u>C</u>ambodia, <u>J</u>anuary
23. <u>INS</u>
24. <u>C</u>orvino, <u>S</u>upertire
25. <u>U</u>nited <u>S</u>tates, <u>A</u>laska

ACTIVITY 3-2, page 43

Review your sentences with a classmate. Give yourself 1 point for each correct sentence.

UNIT 4

CHECKPOINT 4-1, page 44

1. apostrophe
   question mark
2. apostrophe
   exclamation point
3. dash
   exclamation point
4. comma
   comma
   period
5. question mark
6. ellipsis marks
   apostrophe
   exclamation point
7. apostrophe
   period
8. colon
   comma
   period
9. quotation mark
   apostrophe
   period
   comma
   period
   quotation mark
10. hyphen
    exclamation point
11. exclamation point

CHECKPOINT 4-2, page 47

1. can't
2. Gipson:
3. What's
4. games:
5. 1:03

CHECKPOINT 4-3, page 49

1. dollars—
2. Guard—/Shores—
3. Portland,
4. Reading, writing,
5. said,

CHECKPOINT 4-4, page 50

1. development . . .
2. Wow!
3. the . . .
4. Fire! Fire!
5. Wait!

CHECKPOINT 4-5, page 51

1. (1)/(2)/(3)
2. Three-fourths
3. well-known
4. (Megan/Liza)
5. self-satisfied

CHECKPOINT 4-6, page 52

1. Mr. Reynolds.
2. song?
3. 1985?
4. A.M./P.M.
5. job?

CHECKPOINT 4-7, page 54

1. "Be/attitude."
2. talented;
3. riser;

4. "How/happen?"
5. late;

ACTIVITY 4-1, page 55

(Each set of parentheses and quotation marks count as 2 points.)

1. 3	17. 2
2. 1	18. 1
3. 7	19. 2
4. 1	20. 3
5. 2	21. 4
6. 2	22. 6
7. 2	23. 6
8. 1	24. 0
9. 1	25. 0
10. 1	26. 1
11. 0	27. 1
12. 2	28. 3
13. 4	29. 0
14. 5	30. 2
15. 3	31. 1
16. 3	32. 1

ACTIVITY 4-2, page 56

1. You're/alone.
2. working—/option.
3. he's/are: secretarial, accounting, and sales.
4. skills: (1) spelling, (2) math, and (3) writing skills.
5. you'll/away.
6. full-time/part-time work?
7. response, "No, you're/for,"/ego.
8. self-confidence/appearance.
9. time, patience, and hard work.
10. Congratulations!/hired.
11. continued . . ./respond.
12. Hooray!/test.
13. didn't/job; however,/experience.
14. 14,/8:30 A.M.
15. re-entering/work force.

UNIT 5

CHECKPOINT 5-1, page 62

1–10 Review your sentences with a classmate. Give yourself 1 point for each correct sentence. Subjects and verbs must be underlined, too.

CHECKPOINT 5-2, page 64

Give yourself 1 point for each correct sentence.

1. Her parents will help her buy a new car; however, she will pay for the car insurance.
2. She has rented an apartment; therefore, she wants a roommate to share expenses.
3. Jason completed the job application, and he took a math and grammar test.
4. He could operate the computer; otherwise, he would not meet one requirement of the job.
5. The work hours are flexible; however, he will have to work one weekend a month.

CHECKPOINT 5-3, page 67

Give yourself 1 point for each correct answer.

1. I	2. he
3. I	4. he
5. seems	6. has
7. is	8. go
9. surprises	10. has

CHECKPOINT 5-4, page 68

Give yourself 1 point for each correct answer.

1. b
2. b
3. b
4. a
5. b

ACTIVITY 5-1, page 70

1–6 Review your sentences with a classmate. Give yourself 1 point for each correct sentence.

ACTIVITY 5-2, page 74

Give yourself 1 point for underlining the correct subject and for underlining the correct verb. Give yourself 1 point for the correct number—singular or plural.

1. plural/They are
2. singular/Mrs. Stein was promoted
3. singular/waiter carries
4. plural/custodians wash

5. singular/<u>Yuan</u> <u>writes</u>
6. plural/<u>We</u> <u>were</u> <u>asked</u>
7. singular/<u>she</u> <u>walks</u>
8. plural/<u>Gina</u>/<u>Armando</u> <u>drive</u>
9. singular/<u>building</u> <u>has</u>
10. singular/<u>supervisor</u> <u>explains</u>

UNIT 6

CHECKPOINT 6-1, page 77

Give yourself 1 point for each sentence underlined correctly.

1. TS   Employability skills are necessary for any job in every business and industry.
   ES   Remember, employability skills are needed in *every* job.
2. TS   Recycling is one way we can help save our environment.
   ES   Recycling reduces air and water pollution and is one way to save our environment.
3. TS   A detailed auto maintenance schedule can save you a lot of money.
   ES   Regular car care and detailed maintenance will result in fewer major repairs.
4. TS   How smart are you when it comes to budgeting your income and handling money matters?
   ES   By creating a budget, you will be managing your income effectively and wisely.

CHECKPOINT 6-2, page 78

Give yourself 2 points for each correct answer.
1. c
2. e
3. d

CHECKPOINT 6-3, page 81

Give yourself 1 point for each correct number.

1. 5	3. 2	5. 6	7. 3
2. 4	4. 9	6. 1	8. 8

ACTIVITY 6-1, page 82

Each paragraph should have a topic sentence, at least two sentences in the body, and an ending sentence. Give yourself 1 point for each Yes answer.

ACTIVITY 6-2, page 83

Give yourself 2 points for each correct answer.
1. e
2. c
3. b
4. c

UNIT 7

CHECKPOINT 7-1, page 87

There should be a check mark in each Yes space. Give yourself 1 point for each Yes answer.

CHECKPOINT 7-2, page 89

1. b
2. a

CHECKPOINT 7-3, page 92

1. Yes
2. Yes
3. Yes
4. Yes
5. Yes

ACTIVITY 7-1, page 93

1. b
2. c
3. a
4. c
5. a

ACTIVITY 7-2, page 95

There should be a check mark in each Yes space. Give yourself 1 point for each Yes answer.

UNIT 8

CHECKPOINT 8-1, page 102

Personal Information
Give yourself 1 point for each item.
1. Name
2. Address
3. Telephone number
4. Social Security number

5. Date of birth
6. Driver's license number

CHECKPOINT 8-2, page 103

Educational Background
Give yourself 1 point for each item.
1. Name of school
2. Address
3. Dates attended

CHECKPOINT 8-3, page 104

Specialized Courses and Certificates
Give yourself 1 point for each item.
1. Name of school
2. Name of specialized course or certificate
3. Date(s)

CHECKPOINT 8-4, page 105

Extracurricular Activities and Organizations
Give yourself 1 point for each item.
List of extracurricular activities
Name of organization(s) or group(s)

CHECKPOINT 8-5, page 105

Honors and Awards
Give yourself 1 point for each item.
Name of honor(s) or award(s)

CHECKPOINT 8-6, page 106

Work History
Give yourself 1 point for each item.
Each paid job should have
1. Name of employer
2. Address
3. Job title or job duties
4. Dates employed
5. Supervisor and telephone number
6. Starting and final salary
7. Reason for leaving

CHECKPOINT 8-7, page 107

Skills and Abilities
Give yourself 1 point for each item.
List of each special skill and ability

CHECKPOINT 8-8, page 107

Interests, Talents, and Aptitudes
Give yourself 1 point for each item.
List of interests, talents, and aptitudes

CHECKPOINT 8-9, page 108

Career Objective
Give yourself 1 point for each item.
1. Name(s) of jobs qualified for
2. Career goal

CHECKPOINT 8-10, page 109

References
Give yourself 1 point for each item.
Each reference should have
1. Name and title
2. Address
3. Telephone number

ACTIVITY 8-1, page 111

1. g	2. d
3. e	4. a
5. b	6. f
7. c	

UNIT 9

CHECKPOINT 9-1, page 112

1. False	4. False
2. True	5. False
3. True	

CHECKPOINT 9-2, page 116

1. Your name
2. Street or P.O. box
3. City, state, ZIP Code
4. Area code and telephone number

CHECKPOINT 9-3, page 117

1. Your Career Objective

CHECKPOINT 9-4, page 117

Give yourself 10 points. Subtract 1 point for each misspelled word and each date left out.

CHECKPOINT 9-5, page 117

Give yourself 10 points. Subtract 1 point for each misspelled word and each date left out.

CHECKPOINT 9-6, page 117

Give yourself 1 point for each special skill.

CHECKPOINT 9-7, page 118

Give yourself 10 points. Subtract 1 point for each misspelled word and each incomplete name and address.

CHECKPOINT 9-8, page 119

1. 1987-89-Automotive Technical Institute
        Detroit, Michigan
        Received Automotive
            Mechanic Certificate
2. 1986-87-Yee's Foreign Car Repair
        Auto Mechanic Assistant

ACTIVITY 9-1, page 120

1. Personal Information
2. Objective
3. Education
4. Experience
5. Skills and Abilities
6. References

ACTIVITY 9-2, page 120

1. <u>V</u>ocational
   <u>O</u>klahoma
   <u>C</u>onstruction P<u>r</u>ogram
2. Mana<u>g</u>er
   <u>E</u>mporium
   Stre<u>e</u>t
   <u>OR</u>
   No area code
3. <u>Mr</u>. <u>O</u>saki
   <u>A</u>pprenticeship
   <u>S</u>uite
   <u>E</u>ugene
   Incomplete phone number

UNIT 10

CHECKPOINT 10-1, page 124

1. Did you print plainly? Yes ___ No ___
2. Did you write your last name first? Yes ___ No ___
3. Did you include your ZIP Code? Yes ___ No ___
4. Did you include the area code with your telephone number? Yes ___ No ___
5. Is your Social Security number accurate? Yes ___ No ___

Give yourself 1 point for each Yes answer.

CHECKPOINT 10-2, page 125

1. Did you answer three items on the first line? Yes ___ No ___
2. Did you answer either Section B or Sections A and B? Yes ___ No ___

Give yourself 1 point for each Yes answer.

CHECKPOINT 10-3, page 126

1. Did you print plainly? Yes ___ No ___
2. Do the addresses include street, city, state, and ZIP Code? Yes ___ No ___

Give yourself 1 point for each Yes answer.

CHECKPOINT 10-4, page 128

1. Is your current job listed first? If not working, is your last job listed first? Yes ___ No ___
2. For each job listed, was the following completed?
   a. Dates employed include month and year Yes ___ No ___
   b. Current or last position Yes ___ No ___
   c. Starting and final salary Yes ___ No ___
   d. Address including city, state, and ZIP Code Yes ___ No ___
   e. Telephone number Yes ___ No ___
   f. Duties Yes ___ No ___
   g. Reason for leaving Yes ___ No ___

Give yourself 1 point for each Yes answer.

CHECKPOINT 10-5, page 129

1. Did you include at least two references? Yes ___ No ___
2. Does each reference address include city, state, and ZIP Code? Yes ___ No ___
3. Is the telephone number included for each reference? Yes ___ No ___

Give yourself 1 point for each Yes answer.

CHECKPOINT 10-6, page 130

1. Did you sign the
   application?   Yes ___ No ___
2. Did you date the
   application?   Yes ___ No ___

Give yourself 1 point for each Yes answer.

ACTIVITY 10-1, page 132

1. a	2. b	3. a	4. a
c	d	c	b
		d	c

Give yourself 1 point for each correct
answer.

UNIT 11

CHECKPOINT 11-1, page 136

1. a	2. f
3. g	4. b
5. h	6. d
7. c	

CHECKPOINT 11-2, page 138

1. Does your letter include these parts?
   Return address and
   date   Yes ___ No ___
   Letter address   Yes ___ No ___
   Salutation   Yes ___ No ___
   Closing   Yes ___ No ___
2. Did you use open
   punctuation?   Yes ___ No ___
3. Did you state the
   position you are
   applying for?   Yes ___ No ___
4. Did you ask for an
   interview?   Yes ___ No ___
5. Does your letter look
   neat and attractive?   Yes ___ No ___
6. Did you sign the
   letter?   Yes ___ No ___

Give yourself 1 point for each Yes answer.
Get an extra point if all words are spelled
correctly.

CHECKPOINT 11-3, page 139

1. True	2. True
3. False	4. True
5. True	

CHECKPOINT 11-4, page 141

1. Does your letter include these parts?
   Return address and
   date   Yes ___ No ___
   Letter address   Yes ___ No ___
   Salutation   Yes ___ No ___
   Closing   Yes ___ No .___
2. Did you use mixed
   punctuation?   Yes ___ No ___
3. Did you say thank you
   in the opening
   paragraph?   Yes ___ No ___
4. Did you reaffirm
   your interest and
   availability?   Yes ___ No ___
5. Does your letter look
   neat and attractive?   Yes ___ No ___
6. Did you sign the
   letter?   Yes ___ No ___

Give yourself 1 point for each Yes answer.
Get an extra point if all words are spelled
correctly.

CHECKPOINT 11-5, page 142

1. Does both the return address and
   receiver's address include these parts?
   Two-letter state
   abbreviation   Yes ___ No ___
   ZIP Code   Yes ___ No ___
2. Are addresses in all
   capital letters with
   no punctuation?   Yes ___ No ___
3. Is the letter folded
   correctly?   Yes ___ No ___

Give yourself 1 point for each Yes answer.

ACTIVITY 11-1, page 143

1. Does your letter include these parts?
   Return address and
   date   Yes ___ No ___
   Letter address   Yes ___ No ___
   Salutation   Yes ___ No ___
   Closing   Yes ___ No ___
2. Did you use open
   punctuation?   Yes ___ No ___
3. Did you state the
   position you are
   applying for?   Yes ___ No ___

4. Did you ask for an
   interview?   Yes ___ No ___
5. Does your letter look
   neat and attractive?   Yes ___ No ___
6. Did you sign the
   letter?   Yes ___ No ___

Give yourself 1 point for each Yes answer.
Get an extra point if all words are spelled
correctly.

ACTIVITY 11-2, page 143

1. Does both the return address and
   receiver's address include these parts?
   Two-letter state
   abbreviation   Yes ___ No ___
   ZIP Code   Yes ___ No ___
2. Are addresses in all
   capital letters with
   no punctuation?   Yes ___ No ___
3. Is the letter folded
   correctly?   Yes ___ No ___

Give yourself 1 point for each Yes answer.

UNIT 12

CHECKPOINT 12-1, page 148

Each section should have one item
marked. Give yourself 4 points.

CHECKPOINT 12-2, page 149

1. Does Line G equal the
   total of Lines A
   through F?   Yes ___ No ___
2. Is the first name
   written first?   Yes ___ No ___
3. Is the home address
   included?   Yes ___ No ___
4. Are the city and state
   included?   Yes ___ No ___

5. Is the ZIP Code
   included?   Yes ___ No ___
6. Are there nine digits
   in the Social Security
   number?   Yes ___ No ___
7. Is one box marked for
   marital status?   Yes ___ No ___
8. Is Line 4 the same
   number written in
   Line G?   Yes ___ No ___
9. Is Line 7 marked?   Yes ___ No ___
10. Is the form signed?   Yes ___ No ___
11. Is the form dated?   Yes ___ No ___
12. Is information printed
    except for signature?   Yes ___ No ___

Give yourself 1 point for each Yes answer.

CHECKPOINT 12-3, page 152

1. Is the last name
   written first?   Yes ___ No ___
2. Is the birth name
   included?   Yes ___ No ___
3. Is the address
   included?   Yes ___ No ___
4. Are the city and state
   included?   Yes ___ No ___
5. Is the ZIP Code
   included?   Yes ___ No ___
6. Is the date of birth
   included?   Yes ___ No ___
7. Are boxes 1, 2, or 3
   marked?   Yes ___ No ___
8. Is the form signed?   Yes ___ No ___
9. Is the form dated?   Yes ___ No ___
10. Is the information
    printed except for the
    signature?   Yes ___ No ___

Give yourself 1 point for each Yes answer.

CHECKPOINT 12-4, page 155

Give yourself 10 points. Subtract 1 point for each error.

```
┌─────────────────────────────────────────┐
│           SPORTS UNLIMITED               │
│             458 PARK ST.                 │
│         BOSTON, MA  02107-1234           │
│            (617) 555-3846                │
│                                          │
│              DATE Current 19 Date        │
│  SOLD TO  Barry Cowan                    │
│  ADDRESS 1248 Oak St., Denver, CO 80232- │
│  SHIP TO                      1248       │
│  ADDRESS                                 │
│                                          │
│ QUANTITY │ DESCRIPTION │ PRICE │ AMOUNT  │
│    1     │ J. V. Sports Shoes │  │ 29 95 │
│          │             │       │         │
│          │             │       │         │
│          │             │  TAX  │  1  80  │
│          │             │ TOTAL │ 31  75  │
│  CASH    │ CHARGE │ SOLD BY  KYI         │
│          │   ✓    │                      │
└─────────────────────────────────────────┘
```

ACTIVITY 12-1, page 156

1. Dameron
2. 546-27-6831
3. Single
4. Tampa, Florida
5. 1

ACTIVITY 12-2, page 157

1. December 15, 19—
2. Rachel Acosta
3. Cash
4. four; remember the two pairs of socks
5. $1.80

UNIT 13

CHECKPOINT 13-1, page 160

1. Arnold Stein
2. Parking Lot C Resurfacing
3. March 8
4. Parking Lots A or B, street parking
5. ef

CHECKPOINT 13-2, page 160

1. Ms. Lilly Dong
2. Vacation
3. No
4. Your name
5. Yes

CHECKPOINT 13-3, page 162

1. mail carrier
2. fire fighter
3. enclosed
4. work force
5. thank you
6. we think
7. because
8. humanity
9. flight attendant
10. supervisor

ACTIVITY 13-1, page 164

1. No	2. Yes
3. No	4. No
5. Yes	

ACTIVITY 13-2, page 164

1. Co-workers, employees, or names of specific people
2. Car pool
3. Your name
4. Yes
5. Yes

ACTIVITY 13-3, page 166

1. **Everyone** would be better off if our air was not polluted.
2. She applied for a position as a **mail carrier.**

3. The **fire fighter** worked 24-hour shifts.
4. Ask the **flight attendant** for a blanket.
5. The **supervisor** praised his employees.

UNIT 14
CHECKPOINT 14-1, page 170

Give yourself 1 point for each correct answer.

1. Mr. Isiah Walton, General Manager
   Las Posas Auto Parts
   4987 Las Posas Street
   Chicago, IL 60605-7243

   Dear Mr. Walton

2. Mrs. Nan Ott
   Personnel Department
   American Electronics Corporation
   765 Moana Blvd., Suite 34
   Honolulu, HI 96813-7374

   Dear Mrs. Ott:

CHECKPOINT 14-2, page 172

1. NE
2. WV
3. TN
4. SD
5. NY
6. OK
7. MT
8. AK
9. IA
10. MS

CHECKPOINT 14-3, page 174

1. Horizontal center, after letterhead
2. four or five (Ms. Anne Rossi, Sales Representative can be on one or two lines)
3. Dear Ms. Rossi
4. XRT Model 348
5. one blank or double-space
6. Horizontal center, double-space below body
7. Reference initials

ACTIVITY 14-1, page 175
1. No
2. Yes
3. No
4. Yes
5. Yes
6. Yes
7. No
8. No
9. Yes
10. No

ACTIVITY 14-2, page 176
1. b
2. b
3. a
4. b
5. c

UNIT 15
CHECKPOINT 15-1, page 183

A short-term and long-term goal is written in at least 10 categories. Give yourself 1 point for each box completed.

CHECKPOINT 15-2, page 187

The goal category and short-term goal are filled in. All four questions are answered. Specific things you will do are listed in Question 4. Give yourself 1 point for each answer to Questions 1-4. Give yourself 1 point for the category and short-term goal.

ACTIVITY 15-1, page 188

All four questions are answered. Specific things you will do are listed in Question 4. Give yourself 1 point for writing the category and long-term goal. Give yourself 1 point for each answer to the four questions.

PERSONAL PROGRESS RECORD

Name: _____

UNIT 1: The Sentence and Its Parts

Exercise	Score
Checkpoint 1-1	_____
Checkpoint 1-2	_____
Checkpoint 1-3	_____
Checkpoint 1-4	_____
Checkpoint 1-5	_____
Checkpoint 1-6	_____
Checkpoint 1-7	_____
Activity 1-1	_____
Activity 1-2	_____
Activity 1-3	_____
Total	_____

HOW ARE YOU DOING?

52 or better	Excellent
49–51	Good
46–48	Fair
Less than 46	See Instructor

UNIT 2: Parts of Speech

Exercise	Score
Checkpoint 2-1	_____
	_____
Checkpoint 2-2	_____
Checkpoint 2-3	_____
Checkpoint 2-4	_____
Checkpoint 2-5	_____
Checkpoint 2-6	_____
Checkpoint 2-7	_____
Checkpoint 2-8	_____
Checkpoint 2-9	_____
Activity 2-1	_____
Activity 2-2	_____
Activity 2-3	_____
Total	_____

HOW ARE YOU DOING?

116 or better	Excellent
110–115	Good
104–109	Fair
Less than 104	See Instructor

UNIT 3: Capitalization

Exercise	Score
Checkpoint 3-1	_____
Checkpoint 3-2	_____
Checkpoint 3-3	_____
Checkpoint 3-4	_____
Activity 3-1	_____
Activity 3-2	_____
Total	_____

HOW ARE YOU DOING?

182 or better	Excellent
175–181	Good
165–174	Fair
Less than 165	See Instructor

213

UNIT 4: Punctuation

Exercise	Score
Checkpoint 4-1	_____
Checkpoint 4-2	_____
Checkpoint 4-3	_____
Checkpoint 4-4	_____
Checkpoint 4-5	_____
Checkpoint 4-6	_____
Checkpoint 4-7	_____
Activity 4-1	_____
Activity 4-2	_____
Total	_____

HOW ARE YOU DOING?
170 or better	Excellent
165–169	Good
160–164	Fair
Less than 160	See Instructor

UNIT 5: Writing Sentences

Exercise	Score
Checkpoint 5-1	_____
Checkpoint 5-2	_____
Checkpoint 5-3	_____
Checkpoint 5-4	_____
Activity 5-1	_____
Activity 5-2	_____
Total	_____

HOW ARE YOU DOING?
56 or better	Excellent
51–55	Good
46–50	Fair
Less than 46	See Instructor

UNIT 6: Paragraphs

Exercise	Score
Checkpoint 6-1	_____
Checkpoint 6-2	_____
Checkpoint 6-3	_____
Activity 6-1	_____
Activity 6-2	_____
Total	_____

HOW ARE YOU DOING?
24 or better	Excellent
20–23	Good
16–19	Fair
Less than 16	See Instructor

UNIT 7: Notes and Messages

Exercise	Score
Checkpoint 7-1	_____
Checkpoint 7-2	_____
Checkpoint 7-3	_____
Activity 7-1	_____
Activity 7-2	_____
Total	_____

HOW ARE YOU DOING?
42 or better	Excellent
41	Good
40	Fair
Less than 40	See Instructor

UNIT 8: A Personal Profile

Exercise	Score
Checkpoint 8-1	_____
Checkpoint 8-2	_____
Checkpoint 8-3	_____
Checkpoint 8-4	_____
Checkpoint 8-5	_____
Checkpoint 8-6	_____
Checkpoint 8-7	_____
Checkpoint 8-8	_____
Checkpoint 8-9	_____
Checkpoint 8-10	_____
Activity 8-1	_____
Total	_____

HOW ARE YOU DOING?

25 or better	Excellent
24	Good
23	Fair
Less than 23	See Instructor

UNIT 9: Resume

Exercise	Score
Checkpoint 9-1	_____
Checkpoint 9-2	_____
Checkpoint 9-3	_____
Checkpoint 9-4	_____
Checkpoint 9-5	_____
Checkpoint 9-6	_____
Checkpoint 9-7	_____
Checkpoint 9-8	_____

Activity 9-1	_____
Activity 9-2	_____
Total	_____

HOW ARE YOU DOING?

60 or better	Excellent
55–59	Good
50–54	Fair
Less than 50	See Instructor

UNIT 10: Job Applications

Exercise	Score
Checkpoint 10-1	_____
Checkpoint 10-2	_____
Checkpoint 10-3	_____
Checkpoint 10-4	_____
Checkpoint 10-5	_____
Checkpoint 10-6	_____
Activity 10-1	_____
Total	_____

HOW ARE YOU DOING?

27 or better	Excellent
26	Good
25	Fair
Less than 25	See Instructor

UNIT 11: Personal/Business Letters

Exercise	Score
Checkpoint 11-1	_____
Checkpoint 11-2	_____
Checkpoint 11-3	_____
Checkpoint 11-4	_____
Checkpoint 11-5	_____
Activity 11-1	_____
Activity 11-2	_____
Total	_____

HOW ARE YOU DOING?
36 or better	Excellent
35	Good
34	Fair
Less than 34	See Instructor

UNIT 12: Forms

Exercise	Score
Checkpoint 12-1	_____
Checkpoint 12-2	_____
Checkpoint 12-3	_____
Checkpoint 12-4	_____
Activity 12-1	_____
Activity 12-2	_____
Total	_____

HOW ARE YOU DOING?
40 or better	Excellent
36–39	Good
32–35	Fair
Less than 32	See Instructor

UNIT 13: Memos

Exercise	Score
Checkpoint 13-1	_____
Checkpoint 13-2	_____
Checkpoint 13-3	_____
Activity 13-1	_____
Activity 13-2	_____
Activity 13-3	_____
Total	_____

HOW ARE YOU DOING?
29 or better	Excellent
27–28	Good
25–26	Fair
Less than 25	See Instructor

UNIT 14: Business Letters

Exercise	Score
Checkpoint 14-1	_____
Checkpoint 14-2	_____
Checkpoint 14-3	_____
Activity 14-1	_____
Activity 14-2	_____
Total	_____

HOW ARE YOU DOING?
37 or better	Excellent
35–36	Good
33–34	Fair
Less than 33	See Instructor

UNIT 15: Your Self-Improvement
Action Plan

Exercise	Score
Checkpoint 15-1	_____
Checkpoint 15-2	_____
Activity 15-1	_____
Total	_____

HOW ARE YOU DOING?

28 or better	Excellent
26–27	Good
24–25	Fair
Less than 24	See Instructor